A Continuing Education

A Continuing Education

Samuel F. Pickering, Jr.

*Published for the University of Connecticut
by University Press of New England
Hanover and London, 1985*

University Press of New England

Printed in the United States of America

LIBRARY OF CONGRESS CATALOGING IN PUBLICATION DATA

Pickering, Samuel F., 1941–
  A continuing education.

  1. Continuing education. I. Title.
LC5215.P48 1985   374   85–40492
ISBN 0–87451–353–7

Acknowledgments: "Man of Letters" (1985), "Continuing Education" (1979), "A Thousand and One Classrooms" (1982), and "The Books I Left Behind" (1981) are reprinted by permission from *The Virginia Quarterly Review.* "The Very Thought of Turtles" is reprinted with permission from the May 1983 issue of *Yankee* Magazine, published by Yankee Publishing Inc., Dublin, N.H. 03444, copyright 1983. "Pedagogica Deserta" (1981) originally appeared in *The American Scholar.* "Occupational Hazard" (1979) is reprinted by permission from *National Review,* © 1979 by National Review, Inc., 150 East 35th Street, New York, N.Y. 10016. "Old Things and New Baby" (1982) originally appeared in *Southwest Review.* "Reading at Forty" (1984) originally appeared in *Sewanee Review.* "Unknown" (1984) is reprinted by permission from *Negative Capability.* "Upstairs" originally appeared in the April 15, 1985 issue of *The Kenyon Review.* "Composing a Life" (1985) originally appeared in *College English.*

*For Vicki under whose hands
our children grow greenly loving*

Contents

A Continuing Education

Man of Letters

Occasionally I write familiar essays. When I send them to editors, I usually explain that I am trying to write my way to a new car, adding that I have done well recently and have earned the front half of a station wagon, the automatic transmission, power brakes, and a luggage rack. Of course, that's not true. My essays will never earn me a new car. Besides I am happy with my 1973 Pontiac. Although it is rusting around the edges and the sun has so bleached it that it looks like a tired, old dachshund, it is comfortable and suits me. Other people, though, want to see me in "better circumstances," as a friend put it. After I was towed for the second time last year, he advised me to look at Toyotas, saying they were "splendidly efficient."

Efficiency, however, is not something I think much about. If anything, I am afraid of it. The second time my car broke down was on the Interstate at seven-thirty Labor Day morning. I was headed for a road race in New Haven and wore blue sneakers without socks, jeans that should have been in the rag bag months before, and an orange T-shirt. On the front in brown was a picture of four runners and the inscription "Woodstock 10 K"; on the back "Linemaster America's Foot Switch Leader" stood out in letters four inches high. Some years ago when I broke down on the road with my wife, I had to wait two hours before someone stopped. Although I looked like an escapee from Danbury prison, things were different this time. I got out of the car, and climbing onto the roof, held up my running shoes. The first car along pulled over, and a girl rolled down the window and said, "Going to the race?" "Yes," I answered, "my car stopped." "Nothing to that," she said. "Hop in; John, here," she continued, gesturing to the driver, "is an engineer at Pratt and Whitney; he can fix anything, and after the race will get you going again." In I hopped, and after the race and lunch and some lies about running, John repaired my car, and I drove home feeling good about life and the people who live it.

No, efficiency is not for me. If it were, I would not write familiar essays. Certainly they will never bring me acclaim or money. Years ago when I started, I was naive and hoping to become a big success sent *The New Yorker* an essay on my athletic doings. "A bit too familiar" the rejection said. The flip tone hurt, and for a while I gave up essays and concentrated on scholarly writing. Since I teach English at the University of Connecticut, I feel obliged to delve into things literary and write a fair amount about them. Actually research and academic writing are enjoyable. In fact they are so seductive that frequently months pass without my writing a familiar essay. Becoming an expert in a narrow area is not difficult. I know a lot, for example, about early children's books, and when scholars have questions about Giles Gingerbread or Goody Two-Shoes, they write me. These inquiries appeal to my vanity and make me want to write more. I dream of my little reputation growing so large that graduate students at the best universities will know my name and the Modern Language Association will solicit my opinions on things academic. Because it tempts me to become efficient and concentrate my energy and life, the dream bothers me and I struggle against it. Sometimes the struggle is difficult.

This past winter I went to New York to be interviewed for a post at a big state university. The interview was held in the New York Hilton, one of the hotels hosting the Modern Language Association Convention. Academics bustled about in the hotel lobby, and after the interview as I made my way to the street, a young woman pushed through the crowd and throwing her arms over my shoulders said, "You are the most wonderful scholar; keep up your good work." Before I could think of a witty answer, she kissed me on the cheek and disappeared back into the crowd. "You bet your sweet article in *PMLA* I'll keep it up," I mumbled while I stood on the curb looking for a taxi. New York makes me nervous, though, and I am not very efficient at catching taxis. By the time one stopped for me, I concluded the woman had made a mistake. Since I had not come to New York to attend the convention, I was not wearing a name tag, and although my last book had received some good reviews, my picture did not appear on the jacket. "A case of mistaken identity," I muttered, and beating down the temptation to covet and pursue reputation as a scholar, I decided that the kiss foreshadowed the danger into which academic writing would thrust me. How much better to write familiar essays and remain unknown, I thought, as I rode the bus back to Connecticut and planned an essay on picking up sticks.

I write about the little things of life like starlings and dandelions and picking up sticks. I do so because the little things are about all most people have. None of my friends live romantic lives vibrant with excitement; instead they jog through the quiet byways of ordinary existence with its leaves and laundry, unread newspapers, diapers and Matchbox cars, and Masterpiece Theater on Sunday night. I also write about small things because they bring me letters. I live in a rambling, old-fashioned house; since I will never earn enough from my essays to redecorate it, I have let it decorate me. Big bundles of faded pink roses cover the wallpaper in my study, and on my desk is an old chamber pot, covered like the walls with roses. In it I keep my correspondence, and whenever one of my essays appears in print it overflows with wondrous mail. These letters are not part of the academic world and its momentary intellectual conflicts; they never bring those feelings of cagy rivalry that come over me when I learn that a younger, and perhaps better, critic has published a study of children's books. The letters come from a fresher place. The wallpaper suits them, and they are redolent of simpler lives in a simpler time.

My wife's family owns a farm in Nova Scotia. The farm is in Beaver River, a little town north of Yarmouth on the Bay of Fundy. Vicki and I spend summers there and almost every day take walks with our children through fields or along the shore. The letters come from that world, and as I read them, I drift from words to goldenrod and Queen Anne's lace, salt marshes and peatbogs and patches of blue and green and white as the coast juts out around Black Point before sweeping into Cape St. Mary's. At night Vicki and I sleep upstairs in a dark Victorian bed with a headboard that towers solidly above us. Through the window blows the sea and the wash of stones down the beach. Sleep comes simply and naturally; I don't dream and early in the morning I wake fresh and thankful for life. Like those nights, the letters I receive renew me, and although they do not offer hope for the world in which I work my way for most of the year, they bring happiness and moments in which I forget self and want to give more to life than I receive.

Last spring *Yankee* magazine printed an essay I wrote on the box turtle.* In the essay I appeared as a slow-moving, gentle bachelor, a turtle of a man, alone and out of step with the age. The first hint that the essay was a success occurred when an elder neighbor who had taken little notice of my wife and me when we moved into our house and who I thought resented our children's breaking the morning's quiet, brought us a caramel cake. We invited her in for tea and cookies and conversation meandered pleasantly along until she said, "I read your article in *Yankee* and I have a question." "What's that," I answered. "Well, I really liked the article," she said, "but I want to know if it has any deeper meaning." "No," I replied. "Oh," she said smiling, "I am so glad"; and with that she turned to Vicki who sat beside her on the couch and taking her hands into hers said, "I must get to know you and those adorable little boys of yours better." That day letters began to trickle in about the essay. In September, *Reader's Digest* reprinted it and the trickle became a flood.

Many of my correspondents described their love for, as one called them, "my slow moving hinged friends." Most of the writers were old, and turtles often reminded them of the past. The owner of Timmy, a woman with grandchildren aged twenty-one and twenty-three, wrote that her husband had "been a turtle lover since early childhood when he roamed the mountains near his home at Delaware Water

* "The Very Thought of Turtles" follows next in this book.

Gap." Exercising in a "private plastic bathtub" and dining on lean hamburger, bananas, and strawberries, Timmy led an idyllic life. From October to the first of April, he stayed close to a warm radiator and slept in a tunnel made from pillows. During the rest of the year he spent his time basking in the sun and listening to relaxing music.

In my essay I said that on the road outside my house I had put up signs reading "Box Turtle Crossing. Slow Down." And actually, whenever I see a turtle on or near a highway, I stop, jump out of my car, pick up the turtle, and after guessing which way he or she is going, I carry it across the highway and turn it loose as far from the road as I can. I have done this ever since I was a child. Perched high on my knees in the front seat of our Ford, I would scan the roadside while my parents drove. Sometimes eight turtle stops would break the six mile drive from my grandfather's farm in Hanover, Virginia, to the grocery store in Ashland. Last year, I showed up with stickers on my socks and trousers and slightly late for a talk in Farmington because I had rescued a turtle. I felt guilty, but after I explained what delayed me, the audience clapped and the talk was a success. Still, I sometimes feel foolish when I stop for turtles, or at least I did until my article appeared. Now I know that hundreds of people behave like me.

"I was traveling down a rural highway," Peggy wrote, "when Golda came into my life. She was sitting on the middle line with a paw over her head. She'd been clipped by cars and had several small holes in her shell." Fortunately Golda's shell rejuvenated, and she now lives safely with Cynthia and Helmet, both of whom Peggy saved from callous owners. Peggy discovered Helmet in a pet store. When she asked why there was no food or water in Helmet's aquarium, the owner answered that box turtles only needed water and food "a couple of times during their lives." Infuriated by the man's ignorance, Peggy bought Helmet. Cynthia had led a better if more sheltered existence than Helmet. For five years she had been a child's pet, so much so, Peggy explained, "she has no idea about turtle life. On seeing an earthworm, she dived into her shell and wouldn't come out until she smelled hamburger." Such a creature was not fit for the wild, and when Cynthia's owner became more interested in petting boys than turtles, the girl's parents decided to abandon Cynthia in the park. Peggy did not think Cynthia could survive and took her home as a companion for Golda and Helmet. Cynthia was so pleased by the change that this past year she laid an egg. Peggy promised to write me if it hatched.

Like Peggy people that save turtles usually have more than one, and I received many letters describing "turtlariums." "Since about 1978," Jane wrote from Alabama, "I have been picking up Box Turtles from roads and placing them in my fenced back yard." Although her back yard was only half an acre, Jane said, it contained thirty-five to forty pine trees and supported "a substantial turtle population." During winter the turtles hibernated under the trees and on hot summer days they "spend a good bit of time burrowed down in pine needles." Although turtles themselves are sluggish particularly in the heat, "turtle owners" are lively. "My normal day," Jane recounted, "begins around six thirty at which time I make Turtle Rounds. I usually see three or four at this time. Some are in concrete blocks (the foundation of one end of the fence). Others are munching away at tomato peels or cantaloupes rotting on the compost heap." Compared to some owners' yards,

Jane's was large. In Virginia, George's yard was only twenty by thirty feet and included a four by eight foot fishpond. Happily for the turtles, though, pines and shrubs filled the yard, and worms, snails, and crickets were plentiful. Around the yard ran a board fence under which George had sunk concrete blocks to prevent the turtles from digging their way out. At one time George owned four adults, but one drowned in the pond and another came out of hibernation too early and died. Now he reckoned he had the two remaining adults and two of four babies born in September, 1981.

People who have, as George put it, "a love affair with Box Turtles" are slow and patient, like the turtle itself, and generally seem apart from the bustle of modern living. I imagine the women sitting in rocking chairs on small screened-in porches drinking iced tea and talking about things past, "memories of Pensacola" or "barefoot days on Missouri country roads where I would paddle along in the dust." The men, I see, coming around to the front porch after digging in their gardens. Wiping their hands on their trousers, they sit down, and like George, they laugh and delight in breaking the slow rocking and nostalgia. "Have you ever witnessed their mating," George asked me. "I can tell you," he continued, warming to the subject, "that the act is not exactly earth shaking—nor does it call for athletics, but for endurance it must be tops. I have seen one pair mate for over two hours. And later that same day they were at it again! The female was one of those that died. Did not bother the male at all."

Universities are rarely communities. Both students and faculty are migrants. Even if faculty members spend their entire careers at one school, they, if they resemble me at least, spend much time thinking about going elsewhere. Such thoughts inhibit the growth of those rich sentimental ties that bind a person to people and place. Research and academic writing undermine community and contribute to an individual's isolation. Because the very nature of a specialty is particularity, the expert usually can share little of his research with others. Moreover, publication and reputation make thinking about taking a "better" post at another institution, not merely a dream but a possibility to be considered and forever reconsidered. In contrast writing familiar essays enlarges the sense of community as the writer is touched by the hopes and fears of all kinds and ages of people. Not long ago, a member of my department died unexpectedly. At the funeral we sang "Abide with Me," and as I walked out of the church, I felt loss and was convinced that I was a part of something. The next week a search began for a replacement, and as I thought about the kind of person we could hire, I became upset—not at the department for looking for "new blood" but at myself for being so alone that death would diminish me so little and that I could forget the dead so quickly. In another job, I wondered, would things, even heartache, last longer? Wouldn't other people, then, I almost pled with myself, be a greater part of my life?

I could not answer my questions. I did know, though, that many of the letters written in response to my article on the box turtle stirred feelings which lasted comparatively long. For several weeks I thought about a letter from Boston, written by "a country girl lost in the city." "I can really understand how you feel about turtles," she began, "as I had a baby turtle left with me while a friend of my son's went into the army but he didn't want him back and after

5½ years Squeaky has grown to be 12½ pounds and has gone from a deep ashtray to a punch bowl then to a ten gallon tank to a fifty gallon tank and now has taken over my tub." The country girl had become old, and being feeble and living in a bad neighborhood, rarely left her house. Squeaky was one of the last pleasures of her life. "He is very smart," she wrote, "and lets the water out by flipping over the plug and then stands up and really is fun to watch. He has thrived on cat food and gets a spoon each morning and again at night. He and Princess the cat, the only cat I know that has a pet, she sits on the toilet and watches him and gets very excited if he starts climbing. But he has to go," she continued; "he needs his own kind of life but I've been wondering if he could hibernate and live in water. Please tell me and I'm curious about what you call a box turtle."

A picture accompanied the letter and showed Squeaky pushing a brick about in the tub. Clearly, Squeaky was not a box turtle. He was a snapping turtle, the kind my grandfather said would bite and not let go until there was a thunderstorm. Unfortunately, although the country girl had tamed an aggressive turtle, she could not tame time or circumstance. "Being handicapped," she told me, "I've got to find a home for Squeaky. My son can't help me as he passed away last new year's eve. I'd like to find a place where I wouldn't have to worry about sick minded teenagers catching him and being cruel as they were near here." The teenagers, she said, had caught a turtle and tying a shoelace around its neck hanged it from a fence and used it for target practice, throwing rocks and bottles at it. A policeman discovered the boys and made them cut the turtle down, bury it and even say a prayer. After describing the incident, the old woman said, "I couldn't take it, knowing Squeaky went through this," and she asked me to "find a turtle farm for Squeaky." A farm in the country, she suggested, would be better than one near Boston because fish and ducks were dying in nearby rivers, and she wanted "Squeaky kept healthful."

She gave me her address and telephone number, and although I wrote her I did not do as I should have done: gone to Boston and brought Squeaky back to Storrs and turned him loose in a horse pond. I told myself that I did not go because her letter arrived in the middle of the semester when I was busy grading mounds of undergraduate papers. Of course, my car was also old and liable, I thought, to break down on a long trip. Furthermore, cities made me nervous, and I wondered what would happen if I broke down in Boston. My journey to New York in December was out of character. Until then I had not been to New York during the six years I lived in eastern Connecticut. For that matter I have never been to Boston or Providence and only been in Hartford twice. Like the country girl, I decided, I would be lost in Boston and so I stayed home. Now I feel guilty and suspect that I am lost in a way the country girl is not.

I received many letters from people who were more at home in the past and the country than they were in the city and the present. "I envy anyone the ability to write," a woman wrote from Chicago; "I am just a music teacher and that's all I can do. But I had the most wonderful, talented mother I'd love to tell everyone about. She played piano, was the best cook in seven counties, made hats, ran a switchboard, could mend fences like a trooper. People came from miles around to see her beautiful flowers. Once she walked back in the woods, found a rocky hillside where she planted flowers and small evergreens among the trees, looking down on a big sycamore and a babbling brook. Every time she had the weight of the world on her shoulders, she'd walk back and sit on a rock. Soon her problems disappeared. She could shoot—oh how she could shoot a gun. She'd have me walk up the road behind the fence row hedge, beating the bushes as I went. She walked down the road slightly to my rear—the gun pointed. Any rabbit I scared out of the hedge—ping—she got him on the run. Well, you can see, I could go on and on."

In writing me the woman had herself walked back into a woods, and when she felt better, had come out hesitatingly and sheepishly, wanting to write more yet aware that she had revealed her heart. I was sorry when she stopped describing her mother, and when the letter ended I thought about my own mother who had also been a good shot. When I was growing up in Nashville, Nelson Leasor worked in our yard occasionally. Mr. Leasor was from east Tennessee and was as angular as the Clinch Mountains. He worked only when he felt like it, and my father wanted to get rid of him, telling mother he would never be reliable. Mother disagreed and said, "just you wait." And wait we did until one day when Mr. Leasor knocked on the door and said, "Mrs. Pickering, I'm going home. There is no sense in raking these leaves. The squirrels chew up so many hickory nuts that every load I carry out back is mostly nuts." "That bothers you does it, Mr. Leasor," mother said. "Yes, ma'am," he answered in as contrary a tone as he could. "Well, I'll take care of that," mother said and went to the bedroom and got her shotgun out of the closet. "Mrs. Pickering, what are you going to do," Mr. Leasor asked when he saw the gun. "I am going to get you a little meat for Brunswick stew," mother replied. "You can't shoot that gun in the city," he said. "And who is going to stop me," mother said going out the door, "not you—come along." Mr. Leasor followed quietly and that evening after he finished raking the yard, he carried home eight squirrels. He was not late for work again, and whenever I saw him in later years, even on his deathbed, he would say, "Sammy, I have never seen a woman shoot like Mrs. Pickering. Right in the city—eight shots and eight squirrels and some of them in Mr. Knox's yard."

Maybe in writing about turtles I was unconsciously escaping from my sandy present and searching for solid rock on which I could sit and renew myself. Turtles had once been very important to me. Every summer in Virginia, the children who lived on grandfather's farm and I spent our days catching things in order to win four contests: the lizard, the frog, the locust (cicada) and the turtle. I didn't have fast hands and I never won the frog or locust contests, but I was observant and always found the most turtles. After grandfather died, grandmother sold the farm and moved to a smaller house near the post office and the train station. Although the contests ended, I still searched for turtles. Almost every day I walked north along the tracks towards Fredericksburg. About a mile and a half up the tracks at the edge of a pine woods near a swamp was a real turtle crossing. Attempting to go from one side of the track to the other, turtles would scrape gravel from under the rails and burrow through. Long, slow freights did not bother them, but fast passenger trains often flipped them onto their backs, and before they could right themselves, many were killed by the sun. The sight of dead turtles upset me, and so I saved as many as I could, righting those on their backs and carrying others across the road bed and into the swamp. Those that were dead I took home and let rot. Then I cleaned and shellacked them and put them on a bookcase in my room. I still have one shell. Since 1958 I have kept it in the glove compartment of every car I have owned. Occasionally Vicki suggests taking it out, saying we need more room for maps. I usually answer that since we don't travel anywhere we don't need to carry maps in the glove compartment. In any case I don't want to remove the shell. It is itself, I suppose, a kind of map, a map of my past reminding me where I came from.

Academic readers learn not to take any writing, even the personal essay, as completely autobiographical. In contrast many of the people that wrote me about turtles accepted my essay as entirely true. In the essay I reflected on the turtle's courtship ritual and depicting myself as an aging bachelor, lamented that I had never met an old-fashioned girl like Miss Box Turtle, who responded shyly to her suitor's ardor by retreating into her shell and peeking out "the front door" demurely. Several people took my lovelorn state to heart and tried to cheer me up. "Samuel," one person wrote, "you just keep studying the box shell and learn from his wisdom, and one day the Lord will send you an old fashioned girl and you will live happily ever after." The study of "God's creatures," a man wrote from Iowa, could make up for not having a wife. "I spend happy hours," he said, "watching the birds come to the feeders and in summer love to watch the antics of the many raccoons that pay nightly visits to the patio to get corn, stale bread, and some times marshmellows." "Hope your life will be filled with peace and love," another man concluded; "stay in good spirits. I am sure that someday soon you will meet an old fashioned girl like Miss Box Turtle. God bless you."

I answered every letter I received and tried to write something which would appeal to the reader. I began by describing catching turtles when I was young. Then I became philosophical. The person who moved slow enough to see beauty in the ordinary, who was "a lover of life in all its endless variety," I wrote, would be happier than one who rushed quickly through days in pursuit of wealth or position. Usually I ended by talking about my plans for future essays and said I wanted to write next about the Daddy-Long-Legs. "Where," I wrote, "were Mommy and Baby and Grandma and Grandpa Long-Legs?" It was time, I said, that somebody wrote about the whole family. Not all the letters I received, though, were easy to answer. Unlike scholarly writing which is often abstract and impersonal and which entails little responsibility because it appeals primarily to readers' minds and moves them only to intellectual play, the familiar essay is particular and personal. Because it frequently appeals to and so moves emotions that people act, it forces responsibility upon the writer. In contrast to the footnotes generated by my academic writings, the essay on the box turtle brought me notes from the heart. "Sometimes it takes me a long time to get around to things," a woman wrote, "and some times I am shy about approaching people I do not know. However, I firmly believe that it's never too late to express appreciation, and I wanted you to know how very much I enjoyed your ruminations about the box turtle." "I have never known any," she went on, "but I am sure that is my loss. I think of myself as a quiet woman; I don't go along with rushing around or being assertive. In those respects, I suppose I am like a box turtle too." "I'm frequently late to work in the spring and early summer," a woman wrote from Georgia, "because I'm helping turtles across the road. Leaving earlier doesn't work because then I see more turtles and my boss doesn't understand. My dream is to have a box turtle sanctuary and to have turtle crossings under every U.S. highway. People think I'm weird, but I figure you'll understand." " 'The Very Thought of Turtles,' " she concluded, "was delightful and next spring I plan to put up some turtle crossing signs. The only problem with your not marrying is that you need to produce offspring that will be turtle lovers too."

As letters like this and that from the "quiet woman" began to stream in, I thought I understood, but initially I was not sure how to respond. It "sounds like you are in my fantasy island," a woman from Minnesota wrote; "you kind of reveal yourself as being old fashioned and shy. I personally don't think that being an old fashioned person is a bit dull at all. Maybe it is true to the out going persons but I simply believe that old fashioned people are the most reliable persons that one can trust. They also are the types of persons who can be very interesting, affectate, romatic and the best companion one can find—after you get to truly know them. I myself is very old fashioned person too. I did overcome my shyness in last couple of years, but I always prefer my old ways. I treasure every thing I own such as my own thoughts, my old friends."

In writing familiar essays I suppose I have built a personal fantasy island, far from the main currents of life, a place where each day, as one man put it, seems "one of those wonderfully lazy Sunday afternoons." In answering the letters of those people whose loneliness led them to respond warmly and nakedly to my narrator's isolation, I tried not to break the gentle peace of a Sunday afternoon. The lies which lead to disappointment with our world are everywhere, and if the life described in my essay had not actually been led, I now wanted my correspondents to believe that the emotions behind the essay were true. Initially I told curious friends in the university that I wrote the essay as an exercise in gilding the mundane. Now I hoped my motivation ran deeper and richer. Whatever the case, though, I knew the feelings revealed in the letters were good, and if I could not prolong my correspondents' fantasy of a bittersweet bachelor dreaming of the right wife, I thought that I might be able to substitute another but still decent picture for it. And so in responding to letters like that written by the very old fashioned person, I talked about the pleasures writing brought me and then described the real loves of my life, my family, Vicki and my two little boys, Francis and Edward.

Writing about my family made me happy, but I worried about the effect the transformation of a turtle-loving bachelor into a husband and father would have on my correspondents. I underestimated the letter-writers, and I soon learned there was no reason for anxiety. "Hello Samuel Pickering," one wrote back, "how are you today. I enjoyed your letter and am so glad you have your Miss Box Turtle and the two little boys. I am making items at present for a craft bazaar. I have never made any box turtles, but thought you might like a Teddy Bear decoration to hang in your little boys' bedroom. If they are in separate rooms, let me know and I'll send you another one. Take good care of Miss Box Turtle and the precious little ones. Please write more articles. God Bless."

This letter invigorated me. And in truth almost all the

people who answered my letters said they were eager to read more of my essays. "Where may I find additional pearls of Pickering ponderings," a woman asked lightly, while a man urged me, "don't ever stop writing. I hope your Daddy Long-Legs article will be in *Reader's Digest.*" So did I, and off I rushed to the library and checked out a dozen books. At first all went well, and I was sure I had found the subject for a pearl of an essay. Some thirty-two hundred species of Daddy-Long-Legs lived in the world, I learned; and they were known by a wealth of names, haymakers, harvestmen, and grandfather greybeards. Three and a half centuries ago in England they were called shepherd spiders. In his *Theater of Insects* (1634) Thomas Muffet explained the name, writing "the English call it Shepherd either because it is pleased with the Company of Sheep or because Shepherds think those fields that are full of them to be good wholesome Sheep-pasture." When I realized that this Muffett was the famous entomologist and the father of Patience, most certainly the heroine of the nursery rhyme "Little Miss Muffet," I thought my essay was as good as sold. I even told Vicki that we could afford a radio in our new car and suggested that we visit a few junk shops to see if we could find a second chamber pot to accommodate all the letters that would arrive after the essay appeared. "One with daffodils or violets on it would be nice," I said. Alas, I spoke without knowing enough about the Daddy-Long-Legs. I soon learned, though. The spider, I reluctantly concluded, that disrupted Miss Muffet's snack of curds and whey must have been a shepherd spider. The legs are not the only long thing on the Daddy-Long-Legs. If a person gently squeezes the sides of the male harvestman, down from an internal sack will drop its penis, an organ, I read, "remarkable for its great size, often exceeding the creature's body in length." Although I had not read Freud for twenty years, he came suddenly to mind, and not eager to be accused of "Daddy-Long-Legs envy," I closed the book I was reading. Then I got up from my desk and taking the notecards for the essay into the kitchen dropped them into the trash can. That night I began an academic article on "Liars and Tattle-Tales in Eighteenth-Century Children's Books."

The Very Thought of Turtles

Summer is almost here, and so far everything is fine. There has been lots of rain, and I am not worried about the well going dry. My peas are covered with blossoms, and this spring a neighbor told me how to keep coons out of my corn. "Plant an eight foot strip of buttercup squash around the corn patch," he said, "coons' bellies are tender and they won't cross squash." I followed his advice; the rows are coming up green and every night I dream about September and sweet corn. Best of all, though, not a single box turtle has been hit on the road in front of my house since I put up signs saying "Box Turtle Crossing. Slow Down."

I have watched box turtles for years and have decided we are a lot alike. I never did well in school; teachers even said I was slow, but like the turtle I minded my business and got along. The world would be better if people studied the box turtle. Unlike the Russian Bear or the British Lion, the box turtle is peaceful. He doesn't have teeth and when threatened he does not roar or rear up on his hind legs ready to fight. Instead he just shuts the door, locks his windows, and lies low. Of course, not all turtles behave this way. Snapping turtles are aggressive and when my great-aunt Sallie visited me recently, she brought Oscar her dachshund. Oscar had a fine time whenever he saw a box turtle in the yard. He barked and ran over, and if the turtle were slow in closing, Oscar tried to push his muzzle inside the shell. No cats live here and after a few days, Oscar was a new dog, strutting about and turning up his nose at dry dog food.

Alas, it takes more than box turtles to turn a city dog into a wise, old country dog. After a week Oscar decided that he was too big a fellow for the yard and he began to wander. One afternoon he went over the hill in back to Smith's Pond. A few bass, a couple of mallards, and a ton of snapping turtles live at Smith's Pond. I don't like snapping turtle soup, and since I have been here, nobody has bothered the snappers. As a result they don't stay buried in mud all day but visit in the weeds around the pond or stretch out on stumps in the sun. Oscar must have found a big one who didn't like having his morning nap interrupted. As we sat out in the backyard drinking coffee and talking about coons and squash, Aunt Sallie and I heard Oscar bark joyously. For a moment there was silence; then there was a terrible hullabaloo. Aunt Sallie even says she heard thrashing about. She exaggerates, particularly where Oscar is concerned, and I don't believe her, but then I don't hear as well as I used to. In any case Oscar soon came running over the hill, lickity-split, tail between his legs and yelping "murder." Blood streamed down his nose, and the veterinarian who sewed it up said that except for a hound who got a head full of porcupine he had never seen such damage done to a nose. For the rest of his visit Oscar stayed home. He returned to dry dog food, and every time he saw a box turtle in the yard he came to the back door and begged to be let inside.

My house was built about one hundred and fifty years ago. It is not big or fancy but it suits me, and I marvel at neighbors who sell old houses and move into new raised ranches or capes. "Solar heat, that's what you have to have," a neighbor told me recently explaining why he had taken out a second mortgage. "Besides," he added, "it was time to redo the kitchen in the old place and Rose wanted a Jenn-Aire Range." To tell the truth, I am occasionally tempted by modern conveniences. Often temptation occurs when I am on my way to the toolshed to get the ax to split wood. "Wouldn't it be nice," I think as I sit down on a box of kindling, "to press a button or turn a knob and have a warm house." Usually I sit there, knees akimbo, ax-head on the floor, planning a new house, until turtles come to mind. Turtles are down-to-earth, no-nonsense creatures. Thoughts of turtles get me off the kindling and over to the woodpile.

The man who studies turtles soon loses interest in a new house. For one hundred and seventy-five million years turtles have lived in essentially the same kind of house. The box turtle's shell has only one room, and its clapboard is always painted orange or yellow and brown, yet the turtle is never dissatisfied. Like my place, the turtle's shell resembles a handyman's special. If his roof leaks, the box turtle doesn't call a repairman but lets his own recouperative powers fix things. Unlike the imperial lion or bear, the box turtle is happy with a modest lot. The diameter of his home territory is less than two hundred and fifty yards. His indifference to the wide world brings rewards. He lives longer than almost any other turtle, and there are records of individuals who lived for more than a hundred years.

The box turtle prefers country to city living. In the South he lives in open woodlands and in New England he lives in pastures and marshy meadows. With his house paid for and no worries about repair bills, the box turtle does not work hard and he sleeps from late October or early November until April. He is not choosy about his bed and burrows contentedly into loose soil, sand, or the mud of ponds and streams. When a cold spell sets in, he piles on another blanket of dirt and digs deeper, sometimes going two feet below the surface. In April he comes out of hibernation. Having been asleep so long, he is understandably hungry. Fine sauces mean little to him; he does not pick at his food and almost anything pleases him. Snails, slugs, caterpillars, spiders, crayfish, grasshoppers, millipedes, termites, maggots, flies, frogs, fish, toads, lizards, salamanders, and small snakes can be found on his dinner table. The box turtle does not believe in wasting anything and he will eat dead birds, mice, and shrews. He is particularly fond of berries and vegetables, and during the blackberry season, like a naughty boy standing sheepishly before an empty pie pan, his face and front claws are stained tell-tale black.

Although he never loses his taste for meat, the box turtle eats more vegetables and fruits as he grows older. The turtles around my house enjoy cantaloupes. Although I am particularly fond of them myself, I have quit growing them. Beginning the day with strong language is bad. When I went out in the morning to pick that ripe, dew-covered cantaloupe I had set my stomach on the night before and discovered that a turtle had already eaten it for breakfast, I am afraid I cussed. Still, cantaloupes were a small price to pay for what the box turtle taught me about eating. In my greener days I was a stalwart trencherman. Not long ago, though, the cast iron on my stomach began to rust and I felt bilious. I did not know what to do until I began to think about box turtles one day in the toolshed. Now I feel fine. Like an aging turtle I eat less meat and more fruit and vegetables.

I am a bachelor. Although I once thought about marrying, I have about given up the idea. I am shy, and as Aunt Sallie says, a bit dull. Besides, from what I read in newspapers ladies don't seem to act like they used to. If I met an old-fashioned girl, like Miss Box Turtle, I might change my mind though. Not only is Mister Box Turtle hungry when he comes out of hibernation in April, but he is lonely, and as soon as he has eaten a good meal, he starts looking for a lady friend. He enjoys the pleasures of courting and is a gentleman. When he meets a likely looking lady, he doesn't amble right up and begin talking. No sir, he introduces himself. In truth he is a little vain, but then first impressions are important, particularly, I hear, in courting. He stops about four inches away from the lady and straightens his legs out so he will look his best. As any proper lady should, Miss Box Turtle looks away and goes back into her house. If she likes him, though, she leaves the front door cracked and peeks out. When he knows he has been seen to his best advantage, Mister Box Turtle sticks his neck out as far as he can and raising one leg off the ground, introduces himself. Mister Box Turtle is not a how-do-you-do-today, good-bye-tomorrow suitor. He appreciates old-fashioned pleasantries. Once he senses a spark in his lady's heart, he prances around her gently nibbling her shell. Throughout the courtship Miss Box Turtle remains demure, and later in the summer after she has become Mrs. Box Turtle, she still maintains propriety. When the time comes to make a nest, she makes it alone in the evening. Some things, she knows, are best done in private. Mister

Box Turtle is not allowed to be present when she lays her eggs, unlike, I understand, what goes on around here when like as not the husband, loaded down with a camera and even a tape recorder, will be in the delivery room with his wife.

I get up early in the morning, but around lunchtime I begin to yawn and every afternoon, I take a long nap on the settee in the parlor. Aunt Sallie told me I needed "get up and go." She said I probably had a thyroid problem and she advised me to go back to the city with her and see her doctor. I have been accused of not being ambitious before. That doesn't bother me, but I am sensitive about my health, and what Aunt Sallie said about my thyroid worried me. For several days I went out to the toolshed to be alone and think about things. I had almost fretted myself into sickness and going to Aunt Sallie's doctor when box turtles came to mind. If I had thyroid trouble, I thought, so did box turtles. Like me they get up early, and about noon they start yawning, particularly on hot days. Although they don't stretch out in the parlor, they do the next best thing and doze under a cool log in the woods. In really dry weather, they don't even think about work and spend mornings and afternoons napping in mudholes and bogs. The very thought of box turtles freshened my thyroid, and feeling wonderful, I went back into the house and had a long, untroubled sleep.

Aunt Sallie accused me of being as bad as her Uncle Herbert who never did a lick of work in his life. Maybe she is right—I wonder if Uncle Herbert liked box turtles. Anyway Aunt Sallie is back in the city. Last week she wrote that she and Oscar weren't coming next summer unless I did something about the turtles. She said she had read a book about turtles and did I know, she asked, that "box turtles have chiggers." I didn't know it, but occasionally I do have to scratch. Still, chiggers are a minor irritant compared to the things that itch people who don't grow wise studying turtles.

Continuing Education

I am the best unemployed teacher in the country. When I taught a course, Dartmouth rented the Knights of Columbus meeting hall. Students followed me like canine gentlemen followed Fifi in the spring—that is before the milk truck ran over her. I'm so nice I pour rose water on toads and sprinkle cologne on copperheads. I am the walking Sermon on the Mount. Not only that—I am almost normal. I help children cross streets and kiss old ladies. I am a latent athlete and watch Monday night football. Yet I'll never teach again. I'll remain unemployed because I refuse to endure any more interviews. I haven't been burned; I've been cindered. I haven't been whipped; I've been minced. This all started in 1970 when I was a fuzzy-cheeked graduate student at Princeton.

The first school that interviewed me was a small college in Ohio. In the beginning things went well. The school had obviously fallen on hard times, but aside from shuddering at the leafy campus, I was gracious and danced about exclaiming "everything's all right with the one-horse shay." I first realized, however, that I was not for that bucolic place over cocktails. When I expressed reservations about a distinguished critic, a fat kook wrapped in beads pranced to his toes and waving a finger at my nose snapped "You, sir, are an ignoramus." Thinking that such familiarity must be an honored local custom, I responded in kind. After elevating my middle finger with solemn dignity, I informed the spangled sausage that if he did not sit down I would kick him in the bottom and he would suffer massive brain damage. After this sparkling exchange, conversation paused and a gaggle of faculty members rushed honking to the bar and dove deep seeking cool intoxication. By the end of the evening, the group resembled Episcopalians on a church picnic: all were possessed by spirits.

I spent that night in the college guest house, a clapboard Victorian eggshell. Towering oaks framed it, and it seemed far from the modern world. Unfortunately, the college chapel was next door, and as I crawled into bed, I realized that the thunder rolling through my head came from without, not from within. Students had erected a loudspeaker system on the chapel steps and were reading the names of the American soldiers killed in the Vietnam War. Morpheus himself could not have slept. All the long night "John Henry Smith" and "John Thomas Smith" crashed around the walls and frightened every lamb I tried to count. By the time rosy-fingered dawn tiptoed over the horizon, I was red in throat and purple in eye. Not even a bucket of coffee could stir me; and at nine o'clock when I met the president, I settled into a chintz-covered chair under a portrait of John Crowe Ransom and promptly fell asleep.

Lunch with a senior member of the English department seemed to go better, however. The man obviously wanted me to join the small talk as he left every third sentence unfinished. I picked up the dangling conversational threads, carried them forward, and wound them about a spool. By dessert, we, I thought, had spun a rounded conversation; and I fairly skipped back to the chairman's house. Alas, things are not what they seem and life is full of troubles. The chairman asked me if I enjoyed the lunch, saying he

hoped my host's speech impediment had not put me off.
"What speech impediment?" I asked. "You must have
noticed it, you know," the chairman answered, "the poor
man cannot finish any speech longer than three sentences."
"And," he added, "it infuriates him when someone completes sentences for him." "Oh," I said, thinking the chairman would make a terrible farmer, shutting the barn door
long after the grey mare ran off with the mule. Just at the
time, however, when the mare and her long-eared lover had
broken into the chairman's house and were eating every
antimacassar in sight, the chairman interrupted my reverie,
saying, "Your plane doesn't leave for four hours. What
shall we do? Shall we watch the baseball game on television?" "And," he continued as he turned the television
on, "have a roguish apple—from the tree in the back yard,
yon know." "Paradise Regained," I quipped while visions
of serpents coiled through my head. After twenty minutes
of intense television, I realized that the chairman intended
to sleep during the game. This, I thought, was the absolute
and utter living end, and I was damned if I would let him
get off with an apple, albeit a homegrown one. Literary
conversation seemed out of place, and so I focused on the
game. When a pitcher threw a fast ball, I said, "Ah, looks
like an aspirin going sideways." A curveball was "the
Egyptian Special complete with mummy spin." No one got
a hit. Batters more poetically "laid the timber to it." The
sleepier the chairman became the more variations I rang
upon this last metaphor. Depending on their fortunes, batters laid oaks, mimosa, sugar maples, weeping willows, and
magnolias to the old horsehide. After forty silent minutes,
the chairman suddenly snorted, looked at his watch, and
exclaimed, "I had better get you to the airport." "What?"

I answered; "my plane doesn't leave for three hours; the airport's only forty-five minutes away, and this game is just Tom Terrific." "No matter," the chairman countered, "we might have a breakdown, you know." One could never tell, he added, what might go wrong with his new car. Within five minutes, we were zinging down the highway twenty miles above the speed limit. I wasn't nervous, however, because the chairman glared at the road and gripped the wheel so firmly that his knuckles were whiter than the eyes of the unfortunate British soldiers who fought at Bunker Hill. We arrived at the airport in record time. After parking his car, the chairman trotted me to the terminal. There we parted. After I checked my bag, I looked outside, and noticed that when the chairman reached his car he began jumping up and down and waving his arms like a dervish. Something must have bitten him. Certainly it was serious because I never heard from him again.

In 1970 I did not attend the Modern Language Association Convention. Instead, before Christmas, I flew from my hometown, Nashville, Tennessee to a Big Ten School in Michigan for an interview. I arrived in the evening and immediately went to a cocktail party where I was seated in the middle of a large, yellow couch. As I bloomed there, members of the English department approached in pairs and asked stinging questions about prelapsarian authors. This was more than mortal flesh could stand, and being reasonable I set about drinking a bathtub full of bourbon. After two hours on the yellow couch, the stopper in my tub became dislodged, bourbon gurgled in the pipes, and putting my arms around the necks of the men on either side of me—one of whom was quoting Italian poetry while the other chanted Gaelic—I brought their heads together, introduced them, and left. The next day I ate lunch in the university cafeteria with twelve strange members of the department. I had a cup of coffee on my tray, and as I sat down the end of my necktie flopped into the cup. I jumped up and the necktie slapped against my shirt, forming a brown pool and almost burning my navel off. I forced a laugh, but no one else grinned and the laughter stuck in my throat like a green plum. Shingles could not have been worse than lunch. No one talked and boredom hung deadly over the meal like Moses with his truths. After lunch, I walked outside into a blinding snowstorm. Six men approached me from the right and said, "so nice to chat with you" and swirled away. The other six approached from the left, said "have a pleasant trip home," and quickly disappeared. I was left alone in the snow. Two months later I received a letter from the chairman. "Mr. Pickering," he wrote, "I cannot tell you what a strong impression you made." If I ever visit Michigan again, I'll turn Ann Arbor into Cold Harbor. The building which houses the English department will resemble my great-great uncle's house which was used as a Union hospital during the battle of Cold Harbor. Blood ran from floor to floor and gathered in puddles in the basement.

I got my own back on the way home, however. Flying out of Detroit was difficult. Snow forced the cancellation of many flights, but I eventually caught Allegheny to Cincinnati. Landing in the thick snow in Cincinnati was frightening. As we descended and the "fasten seatbelts" sign lit up, the man behind me handed me a napkin on which he had written, "When the yellow light says 'Repent' we are in trouble." Mutual terror led to camaraderie; and when we discovered that we were both flying to Nashville, we decided to sit together. At Cincinnati we boarded an American Airlines flight. The plane was almost empty and we had a choice of seats. In 1970 the rear of the plane was not the Smoking Section; it was Cowards' Haven. Comfort lay in resting one's head against the wall of the john; and when my acquaintance and I got on the plane, we strode boldly to the back. Of the last three seats, one had an "occupied" sign on it, and a small box rested on another. We put the box under the seat and sat down. After we had prayed and had almost relaxed, a woman came out of the lavatory and seeing us said, "Oh, darlings, this is my seat and I always travel with my wig next to me. It is in the box." The woman might have talked like Tallulah Bankhead, but people who sit in Cowards' Haven are usually as sophisticated as faculty members in Ann Arbor. Nevertheless, my acquaintance graciously moved up the aisle; the woman put her wig in the seat, and we taxied down the runway. The takeoff was smooth, but when the wheels retracted with their usual thunk, Tallulah grabbed my arm, rolled her eyes and exclaimed "What was that!" "Jesus," I shouted, "the engines fell off!" Dear hearts, you would have thought a little girl had tied a bobcat to a bulldog. Never had I heard such caterwauling. The stewardess scurried back to find out what happened. Later as she mopped the woman's brow, she said to me, "you ought to be ashamed." "Bring me some bourbon," I responded, "and a big cigar."

After my experiences in Ohio and Michigan, I decided not to travel to interviews. This did have drawbacks. In February, 1971, a university invited me to fly to Madison, Wisconsin. When I explained that my wealthy aunt was in the hospital and I was unable to leave Princeton and her bedside, they offered me a post over the telephone, saying I would receive confirmation in two weeks after the completion of bureaucratic formalities. I never heard from them again. Like Don Juan with the ladies, academics enjoy titillating throbbing job candidates. In 1970 the chairman of the English department at a school since made famous by football interviewed almost the entire class of new Princeton Ph.D.'s. He promised everyone a flight to Pittsburgh. The university, however, must have decided that chartering a 707 to fly prospective teachers to the campus was a trifle extravagant because three months later a gross of form letters appeared.

Troubles, as Uncle Remus says, are seasoning; persimmons aren't good until they are frostbitten. Time and cold years in New Hampshire have sweetened the interviews I had nine years ago. Dylan Thomas was wrong. One should not go raging but laughing into the good night. On a bright, clear afternoon, the dean of a distinguished small college in New England asked me, "Mr. Pickering, what earthly use is it to write a dissertation on Sydney Smith? After all, he was a minor figure." Before I could answer, thunder rolled out of the heavens and shook the windows of the room in which we sat. That, of course, ended the interview. Anyone with God on his side would be too controversial for the eastern academic world.

Misunderstandings have determined the tone of many of my interviews. Years ago when naïveté purred in my breast, the chairman of an Ivy League English department interviewed me. As soon as I met him, I noticed his necktie. It was the St. Catharine's College, Cambridge, Boat Club tie, golden Catharine wheels on a claret background. For two years I rowed in the "engine rooms" of assorted St. Cat's boats, and I thought, "Good Lord, I wonder who told him about my rowing days? He must really want me if he has gone to the trouble of finding and wearing 'my' tie. Consequently, I relaxed, scratched, and had a wonderful time. At the end of the interview, I said, "Mr. Saltonstall, I deeply appreciated your wearing the tie." "Huh," he said looking slightly baffled. "The tie," I continued, "I appreciate it." "What tie," he responded. "The St. Catharine's Boat Club tie," I answered; "I appreciate your wearing it in my honor." Silence drifted like a cloud as the chairman glanced first at me then his necktie. Slowly he turned it around, looked at the label, and said, "St. Catharine's Boat Club? No, Brooks Brothers."

Most misunderstandings in the academic world are not sartorial but verbal. There is little that can be misunderstood about a leisure suit. Not long ago when conversation died during an interview with a western school, I brought up one of my hobbies, snakes, and asked if the university had a herpetology department. "Oh, yes," an expert on Virginia Woolf said, "we do, and you should see our greenhouses. The begonias there, I understand, are divine." Now I am a Southerner; people often have trouble with my accent, and if there were such a word as herbetology, one could confuse it with herpetology. But the word does not exist. Alas, since pointing out the error would have been harsh, my interview ended in a bouquet filled with chrysanthemums, columbine, phlox, laurel, lilies of the valley, wisteria, iris, and sowthistle. When I left the room, I felt like the last rose of summer. It goes without saying that I never heard from the school again. Still that misunderstanding was not so bad as the one which occurred when I talked to several faculty members from a state school in Nebraska. For the first half hour, things went too smoothly. Deep in my heart, though, I knew it was only a matter of time until I dropped the molasses jug. The crash occurred when someone noted that I had been a graduate student at Princeton and asked if I had known Henry Razor, who studied electrical engineering. "Sure," I answered, "knew him well. A little bitty shaver but pretty sharp?" My jaw sagged when laughter did not trickle forth, but instead I heard, "Yes, that's him. What's he doing? How is his wife?" For ten minutes I answered questions about Henry Razor, a man I have never seen, and if I ever do see, I intend to shoot. I'll have to kill him because if the lies I told about him ever get back he'll come after me with a shotgun.

It's a pity that western university did not have a herpetology department. If it did I'd be the man to hire. I've been snake-bit so many times I wouldn't even notice a nip by a friendly rattlesnake. Being a typical academic, I'm lazy. Every afternoon a nap attacks me, and I dream of students as sweet as sugar candy. Recently, while I dreamed of committing an indiscretion, the telephone rang. I staggered out of bed and discovered the chairman of a big university in Illinois on the other end of the line. We talked for a quarter of an hour. Only when the conversation ended did I wake up. I could not remember anything we discussed. The next day I wrote the chairman a letter, saying that on coming home from the office my manservant greeted me and said I had received a telephone call. My manservant, I explained, was slightly addicted to alcohol. When tiddly, he often, much to my embarrassment, impersonated me. I gathered, I added, that he had done this in a recent conversation with the chairman. And if the chairman, I wrote, would be so kind as to write me a letter containing the gist of the conversation, I would respond posthaste. Alas, what they say about the mail service must be true, for almost four months have passed and I haven't received the chairman's letter.

Last winter I had several interviews at the Modern Language Association Convention. Not having experienced an interview for several years, I thought things were sure to be better than they were in 1970. I was mistaken. When I walked into the first suite, the past overwhelmed me. The same characters still malingered: Hezekiah the prophet, Stringbean, Four-eyes the pointy-headed boy, Borer the committee worm, Lady Fingers, and the Talking Book. The same question with its agrarian metaphor dominated conversation. "What are your fields?" Why, I wondered, did people confuse me with a Holstein; was I a machine for cropping grass and turning it into milk for adolescents? Was I so tightly fenced in that I could not ruminate at pleasure? The people who interviewed me soon discovered that I was not their kine. After nine years of teaching, I found it difficult to answer the young instructor's intense query, "What do you think of Wordsworth's violet by a mossy stone?" Resisting the urge to be violent with a dusty ashtray, I said that when I saw violets I put weed killer on them—stones I saved for the plumbers when they dug up the front yard to expand the drainage field for the septic tank.

Not all interviews at the MLA convention are held in private rooms. Chairmen who are almost as sophisticated as Billy Whiskers meet job candidates in the communal interview room, a ballroom so crammed with chairs and tables that it resembles a Mah Jong tournament. Thigh to thigh and belly to belly faculty members hover over tables whispering while coveys of new Ph.D.'s flutter in corners waiting to hear their names called: "Would Mr. Hart go to table thirty-eight? Would Miss Frankenberry report to table twenty-six?" An interview in a whorehouse in Port Said would be more dignified. One university scheduled an interview with me in the ball room. I arrived, looked around, pivoted, and leaped out the door and into the bar. Over bourbon I plotted revenge. The university was in a town Sherman by-passed. The next time I travel south the university will wish Sherman had not skipped them. Alongside me that Yankee will look like the Messiah.

While I was doubled over conspiring with my bourbon, a hand slapped my back and "mine is not to reason why, mine is but to hire or die" burst into my ear. I looked up. There teetered an old graduate school companion. Now chairman of an English department at a small southern school, he had spent the day interviewing females in the forlorn hope he could shake HEW off his back. Like a horse leech, HEW had dug in and was swelling fat and comfortable. My friend brought his drink over, sat down, and we soon passed through discretion and into originality. Man cannot, however, live on wit alone, and eventually we found ourselves ordering retsina and dinner in Anatole's Greek restaurant. While visions of the Dodecanese and garlands of vine leaves swam before our eyes, the waiter brought our soup. With the soup, he brought a small bowl containing a clear liquid. We bent over and sniffed it. "Alcohol for the soup," we decided. And since our wine had not arrived, we poured it into our soups. "Only the highly civilized," I said, "brew their first course with alcohol." "Too, too true," my friend responded and broke into song, "Maid of Athens, ere we part, give, oh, give me back my heart." When we finished the soup, our waiter brought the next course. He put it on the table, struck a match, and then reached for the bowl which had contained the clear liquid. When he saw that it was empty, he looked puzzled. "Wants our drink, the greedy beggar," my friend said and then waving his hand added, "Laddiebuck, bring us some more of that liqueur. Like the nectar of the gods, it does wonders for my spirits. What would Byron say? 'Roll on, thou deep and dark blue ocean, roll!' " Regrettably, the waiter's extraordinary behavior stopped the recital before my friend sank the ten thousand fleets. Batting his eyes and grabbing his throat, the waiter danced up and down, making a noise like an automobile and babbled in the unknown tongue. "Marvelous," I exclaimed and fishing a dollar out of my wallet gave it to him, saying, "wonderful, now we really must eat." The waiter refused the dollar; instead he ran back to the kitchen. "Nothing like a Greek restaurant for atmosphere," my friend remarked and we turned to the second course. Suddenly the waiter was back, carrying another bowl of clear liquid. "How thoughtful," I said; but before I could take the bowl from him, he had poured the liquid on the second course. He then lit a match and the food blazed. "Oh, dear," my friend said, "it seems we have drunk train oil." "No matter," I answered, looking up, "here comes the wine."

At nine o'clock the next morning I had an interview with a religious school. Everyone in the room was bushy-tailed— except me. I stood in the need of prayer. Train oil oozed through my stomach, and my head was a roundhouse, filled with steaming engines. The chairman began the interview asking, "Mr. Pickering, what do you think you could add to our department?" Woe is me. Just as he finished the question the boiler of the biggest engine in my roundhouse exploded, and I replied, "Sin." Heat rose about us. Not even Casey Jones could have salvaged the interview.

Atheists can be dealt with, but only the good Lord can save one from Christians. Religious schools are often interested in me because I wrote a book on evangelical religion and the novel. This past spring I travelled to the southwest for an interview with a big Baptist school. Dancing was forbidden on campus, and the faculty handbook stated that teachers could be fired for "gross abuse of trust in faculty-student relationships." And this, brothers and sisters, does not refer to turning grades in late—no, siree, bobtail. When I read the rule, I almost refused the interview. When a university prints such a rule, life must be fundamental.

The interview in Texas was memorable. For two hours the president, vice-president, dean of arts and sciences, and chairman of the English department slapped sizzling questions at me. I fielded everything like Nellie Fox and didn't gump any tobacco juice on second base. Still I am a man that will, on occasion, spit. When asked what I valued in life, I nailed the vice-president at first, replying "grace, wit, dignity, and charity." Holding his bat as steady as Aaron's rod, the dean looked to be a more difficult batter. When he asked, however, what changes I thought would occur in the national morality if the sort of people who went to Dartmouth took over the country, I jumped quickly to my right, scooped up the ball and fired it to first before he got halfway down the line. "Run the country," I answered, "They already do." "But," I continued, "I hope that things will change. Jimmy's being elected president," I stated, "was a sign of better times, the dove carrying the olive twig showing the flood of immorality was over." After this an-

swer, I relaxed and leaned back on my haunches. Right
there's where I swallowed my tobacco and the ball bounded
between my legs. "Do you drink?" the president asked.
"Only for medicinal purposes," I answered. But then, I
continued, I was "highly susceptible to the flu particularly
on Saturday nights." At Christmas, I went on like a bad boy
tying a knot in a cat's tail, I always suffered from scarlatina
while the vapors invariably attacked me in the spring. The
answer ended the interview. Two months later I received a
note informing me that someone else had been hired. That,
though, was a school of true Christians, always thinking of
others. Obviously they didn't hire me because they thought
the southwestern climate would undermine my fragile con-
stitution. A man prey to so many ailments would certainly
be better off in the northeast.

After the interview, the chairman took me to the faculty
club where a dozen members of the English department
joined us for lunch. "Oh, oh," I thought, "the ghost of
Michigan past." All went well though until thinking the
man next to me was a kindred spirit, I described a party I
attended in Vermont before Christmas. Although it was a
divorce party, civilized joy reigned unconfined. There were
no hard feelings and champagne flowed in magnums. Some
months before the husband had left his wife and run off
with another man. The husband had driven up for the party
from Boston with some men friends and had cooked a gourmet meal. His former wife wore a red and green dress and
swept grandly about laughing like Santa Claus while the
couple's small daughter decorated the tree and danced
among her presents like a pixie amid flowers. Alas, what
makes Vermonters warm-hearted gives Texans indigestion.
As I described the party to the man on my left, a man

across the table wagged his head, turned sideways, and bawled, "Divorce?—who got divorced?" The poor man was almost stone deaf. When he spoke, he roared like a cyclone rumbling across the prairie. "It's nothing," the fellow next to me said, "Professor Pickering was just describing a divorce party." "A what!—what did you say," the deaf man hollered and everyone at the table looked my way. "A divorce party," I said; "I was just describing a divorce party." "What—I never heard of such a thing," the deaf man shouted; "did you say someone ran off from his wife?" Around the table ears flapped like turkey buzzards scraping over a litter of drowned kittens. "Yes," I answered realizing that I had to bite the bullet, "the husband ran off with another man." For a moment the deaf man was silent. It was the calm before the storm. "WHAT," he erupted: "what, he did what! He ran off with a man! He left his wife and ran off with a man!"

As the old gentleman said when he dropped the whiskey bottle, "Christmas done come and gone." Conversation flattened out faster than a terrapin trying to cross a busy highway. Eating suddenly became important. For a moment I thought I had discovered those starving Armenians I had heard so much about during childhood. Salad, bread, peas, corn, ham, and tapioca pudding disappeared down gullets with abandon as everyone glanced at his watch and remembered he had an afternoon class.

When I played football in high school, I memorized the signs pasted on the walls of the locker room: "When the going gets tough, the tough get going" and "It's not the size of the dog in the fight that counts, it's the size of the fight in the dog that counts." The child is the father of the man, and I refused to let the Armageddon in Texas discourage me. I gritted my teeth, dug my cleats in, and flexed my forearm. No more schools were going to run over me. Alas, all I heard of the next play was "hup-one, hup-two." The first thing I knew I was flat on my back and my chest was covered with little round bruises. I had been back from Texas only a week when a state university in southern New England asked me down for an interview. Travelling during a New Hampshire winter is not easy. And I did not make the interview the first time it was scheduled. A heavy snow fell the night before, and after driving six miles, I spun around on the highway. If I had continued, the only interview I would have had would have been with St. Peter for a spot in the heavenly choir. Actually, I would have stood a good chance for it because I understand that St. Peter doesn't give a hoot about Affirmative Action. Once they have been washed in the blood of the Lamb, all souls are white and sexless. The resurrection of the body raises some problems, but that is a different matter.

The second time I set out for the interview I rode the bus. I thought the trip would be easy because I could sleep. A Vermont countryman, however, took the seat next to me. In his hand he carried a mayonnaise jar which appeared full of peanut butter and Dr. Pepper. Too tired, though, to be curious, I just glanced at it, then shut my eyes to nap. In my half-sleep I heard the man unscrew the lid of the jar. Suddenly I was bolt upright. From deep within my neighbor came a rumbling that sounded like the harrowing of hell. The nap was over. Seeing I was awake, my travelling companion asked me if I would like a plug of tobacco. He had a jar, he explained, that I could spit into and he shoved the mayonnaise jar into my lap. Although I told him I didn't chew quite so early in the morning, a long conversation began in which I was Horatio to his Hamlet. I could not have bored a word in with a gimlet. From White River Junction, Vermont, to Springfield, Massachusetts, I heard stories that would have stultified Argus. At Springfield my "friend" changed buses and I rushed into the Necessary House to pour cold water on my ears in hopes of reducing the swelling. Lordy, instead of my ears shrinking my eyes bulged. When I walked into the johnny, I thought I had stumbled into a prayer meeting. The room was filled with people. But, I soon noticed, they were doing things I'd never seen done in church—at least not in my church. Like a hound who chased a rabbit into a brush pile but who scratched a polecat out, I turned tail and ran for the kennel.

Although I high-tailed it out of that bus station lavatory in Springfield, I was not very upset. I was a seasoned traveller, and I wasn't going to let the trip ruin the interview. I was interested in the university, and happily the interview was a success. Things went swimmingly, and I reckoned I was about to reach my island kingdom where palms and maidens swayed pendulous at the sound of my voice. Alas, I forgot the shark. Just as I reached the shallows and was dreaming of coconuts, rum, frosted glasses, and ice, HEW and Affirmative Action swam up openmouthed. When they finished, I was ready for the Cat's Meat Man. That was my last interview. I have had enough. I'm not moving out of sight of my own smokestacks. Let chairmen come to me. Until they do, however, I need a job. Maybe I can survive at Dartmouth. A few deaths just before term would help my chances. I have pondered how I could make room for myself. My first plan was to call one of the hard cases I grew up with in Tennessee and ask him to send me three hundred feet of water moccasin. These, I would dump into Turl's Pond, the faculty swimming hole. Although some folks would be snakebit, I counted more on cardiovascular storms to create slots in the faculty. Unfortunately this plan seems doomed. The faculty are jogging. Nowadays nothing produces a heart attack, not even fidelity. Consequently I have begun cruising down sideroads waiting to catch a jogger in full stride. I have chased a few into briar patches but so far I haven't made firm contact. Even worse, these bastards seem born and bred in the briar patch. Not one has been seriously scratched. Still, they had better be careful. My time is coming. If I don't get them here, I'll get them somewhere. Maybe I'll write about them.

Pedagogica Deserta

"Dear Mr. & Mrs. Pikring pleas don't get out to day after 5 in the evening." My wife and I found this note on our door one day in March after we returned from the market. Again rumor predicted trouble in Latakia and we had been warned. We stayed in our apartment that night. This, though, was nothing new; we had not been out on the streets after six o'clock since the end of December.

Each academic year the Council for International Exchange of Scholars sends some five hundred "Fulbrighters" to study and lecture abroad. Most go to Western and Eastern Europe and to, if not the westernized, at least the semi-industrialized, world. A number, however, end up in countries which drive sensitive men to drink before noon. In 1975 I taught English and American literature at the University of Jordan in Amman. This past year I was headed for Ghana. Early in the summer, though, a coup changed my plans, and in September my wife and I arrived in Damascus.

My post was at Tishreen University in Latakia, six and a half hours from Damascus by bus. A town of slightly over two hundred thousand people on the Mediterranean, Latakia is Syria's most important seaport. Before we left the United States, an official in Washington assured us that the city supported a thriving international community. Since the troubles in Beirut, he said, many people had moved to Latakia. The discrepancy between what was described and what we found was great. No native speakers of English lived in Latakia, or at least we never discovered any. Two months after we arrived we met a French couple and they became our only western acquaintances. In the fall many Russians were present in the city. Later, after the Moslem Brothers, the terrorist organization, had assassinated a few, they disappeared into their compound, leaving us alone on the streets.

In September our embassy in Damascus tried to be helpful. Unfortunately they knew little about Tishreen University. Bloodied by violence between religious sects or "insects," as a student mistakenly labeled them in an essay, and stuck in the morass of the Middle East's internecine warfare, Syria itself is not easy to know. Policy can change like the desert wind, and rumor often becomes the only truth.

Classes were scheduled to begin at Tishreen on September 29, so after a week of waiting in Damascus while the embassy tried to find out if Latakia had calmed down after recent riots, we left on a bus. Finding an apartment was easy. The assistant dean asked how much we had to spend, then told us he knew a flat for that price. Not surprisingly, we later learned that the owner's wife was the dean's cousin. Assuredly the dean received a commission, but that was all right, for our landlord was a superb man. He was an Alawite general in the army. Because they are only ten percent of the population, Alawite Moslems from northern Syria had long been treated as second-class citizens by the dominant Sunni majority, some seventy percent of the population. Alawites have a distinct appearance. The backs of Alawites' heads are flatter and less rounded than those of the general Syrian population. This is so, Sunnis say unkindly, because generations of poor Alawites have pushed against the backs of their children's heads in order to get them out of the house and direct them towards Damascus and work. Since good jobs have traditionally been difficult for Alawites to obtain, a disproportionate number made careers in the army. When Hafez al-Assad, an Alawite, became president of Syria in a coup in 1970, the Alawite military came into its own, financially and socially. For a time this did not cause much resentment among the Sunnis. Assad brought much-needed stability, and as schools were built in, and electricity spread to poor isolated villages, the Alawite underclass rose above servantdom. Although a Sunni town, Latakia was surrounded by Alawite villages, and many of my students were villagers seizing the first opportunity for higher education they had ever been offered.

During the past three years, however, resentment of Alawites has grown. Business has been bad and military expenditure awesomely high. Sunni merchants blame Assad for the nation's economic problems and accuse the government and army of being corrupt. Corruption is widespread in the Mideast and Syria is probably no worse than her neighbors. Much Sunni resentment focuses on the Officers' Club. Assad's brother controls it and uses its funds to finance his private army, which has a reputation for savage brutality. To do business in Syria, western corporations make under-the-table contributions to the Officers' Club. One businessman told me about the time he flew from Athens to Damascus carrying forty thousand dollars in his suitcase for the Club. Customs expected him and he was whisked through without his bags being touched. In hopes of destabilizing the government and bringing an Islamic revolution to Syria, the Moslem Brothers have viciously assassinated the Alawite educated elite, whether or not individual Alawites have had anything to do with the government. The disenchanted Sunni majority has not lent the Brothers active aid. On the other hand, the Sunnis have not condemned them either. Since there are few Moslem Brothers, the Sunnis reason that when the government falls they will be able to brush them aside and establish a government of their own. During the past year, hatreds have boiled. The good are silent, and violence has spiraled as the government's secret police have viciously repressed dissent or potential dissent. At times during the year, Aleppo and Hama seemed foreign countries brought back under Damascus's rule only by tank law. "You don't know," a student told me with tears in her eyes; "the people die like rain."

As a general, our landlord was well guarded. Three to seven soldiers lived on the third floor of our building. So when bullets began to fly in Latakia in the spring, we felt almost safe. Growing accustomed to automatic rifles, however, is not easy for a teacher used to nothing more violent than the correspondence column of *PMLA*. Sometimes when we climbed the eighty-three steps to our fifth-floor apartment, a new guard would greet us gun in hand. Frequently visitors received escorts up to our flat. Most took it in stride, but some never returned.

Tishreen University consisted of four faculties: engineering, medicine, agriculture, and letters. For years construction of a new university has been under way. Unfortunately the end is not in sight, and the faculty of letters is, and will be for many more years, housed in a secondary school building just beyond the freight entrance to the port. Unlike the United States, where the shortcomings of education are obvious, Third World countries seem to believe that education will provide the answers to all problems. Consequently governments in such countries, in part because rational dissent is stifled, confuse themselves with the Great First Cause and create universities by decree. The planning comes later—if indeed it ever comes. Tishreen University as it is now was not the gleam that shone in the eye of its creator. In my first day at the faculty of letters, I asked to see the library. The assistant dean showed me an empty room and said, "This is the library, but we don't have any books yet." Since the English department itself was only two years old, the absence of books, although unexpected, did not unduly startle me.

In Jordan, when I was asked what I wanted to teach, I tried to be a good advertisement for my country, and, trusting to the fairness of my colleagues, said I would teach what the department needed. As a consequence, I, like everybody else, taught one elementary and two upperclass courses each semester. In Syria, when queried about courses, I responded as I had done in Jordan. I made a mistake. Dignity is important in Syria, and the accommodating man is often seen as a person of no consequence, to be used and abused at will. First-year classes at Tishreen contained large numbers of students, sometimes two hundred. By the second year many left the university, so that frequently classes had only forty students. In the first semester I taught sixteen hours of courses. Unlike my three Syrian professorial colleagues, as I later found out, I had all first-year students. Six hours a week I taught prose and ten hours a week I taught composition. The chairman, a "specialist" in prose and poetry, taught only second-year students; the assistant dean, a specialist in drama, did the same. Most of the first-year courses were taught by two demonstrators, recent graduates of Syrian universities, and me. This almost graduate-assistant kind of treatment did not initially make me resentful. To obtain a Ph.D., my Syrian colleagues had to work harder, make compromises, and suffer indignities which I knew I could not imagine. Theirs was a real achievement, one that marked them out in Syrian eyes as not merely different from, but better than, others.

My wife and I were the only Americans the majority of my students had ever met, and our style of living was different from that of the Syrian professors. Instead of buying a car or taking a taxi to the university, I walked across town. Unlike Syrian professors, who dressed carefully and kept themselves immaculate by never erasing a blackboard, I wore corduroy trousers, a corduroy sports jacket, and blue topsiders to class. When I erased my own blackboard and got covered with chalk during a two-hour class, students were astonished. Since the lowest workers, porters in the harbor, wore sneakers, my shoes provoked much discussion. Six months after classes began a student told me that he and his friends had been puzzled by my shoes at first. "Every Doctor of Language in the university considered himself a minister," he said, "but you did not. We honor you for your shoes. You come to work." Since I did not appear as a minister, confusion about me and my position lasted throughout the year. In April a student who had attended almost every class but whose English was poor asked me if I were an elementary school teacher in America. Numerous times surprised students told my wife and me, "Americans are so simple and humble."

These students meant to compliment us. Complexity often implied corruption or favoritism. Our accessibility or simplicity or democracy was thought admirable. In contrast to the typical Syrian faculty member, though, I must have appeared as a man who carried himself in a manner unbecoming his position. By doing so I cut the ground from under the faculty member's hard-won achievement and obliquely undermined the hierarchical structure of university life. No wonder first-year courses were loaded on me and I was never consulted about my timetable. I only began a slow burn, however, when I learned that while I taught six days a week, my fellow professors were teaching four.

Although I began to teach on September 29, the chairman did not appear until two and a half weeks later. The third full-time Ph.D. member of the department did not arrive until November. The random appearance of the faculty members was paralleled by the students' attendance. Tishreen was an open university. Many students never attended classes because they held jobs, quite a few teaching in remote villages. Given eight years to pass the required courses, other students pursued relaxed courses of study. As in secondary schools, university education depended primarily upon rote learning. Class discussions, particularly those discussions which raised ideas different from the professor's, were discouraged. At the end of term, professors' lecture notes were mimeographed and sold for seventy-five cents a course. If a student memorized these, he had a good chance of passing. To some extent the notes took the place of assigned texts. The university did not have a bookstore; often local booksellers were not informed what texts were needed for courses until it was too late to order them. As a result, many students never had books, and one member of the department even suggested that books were an unnecessary expense. He proposed that all professors have their notes printed before the lectures started. That way, he explained, students would not have to buy books like *The Old Man and the Sea* or *The Penguin Book of English Verse*.

With new students appearing even on the last day of class, December 24, teaching was a tedious matter of repetition, careful enunciation, and slow speech. In mid-November a latecomer sent me a note asking for help. "The nam of gud. Dear my teacher: Good morning," he began. "I am very later in my lossons," he continued, "pleas help me if you can help me and I promsed you, I will read my lossons in this tim. I wrote this wards becoues the time of examniisoins are not very long. Pleas help me, I need this helps very much. If you help me I am thankful you very much. pleas/pleas/pleas." Although all my students were majoring in English, and this meant taking eight to ten courses in English a year, like this boy few could actually speak much English. In most cases, secondary schools provided them with little background. Of the approximately two hundred and fifty people who taught English in the Latakia school province, fewer than a third were full-time teachers, and these taught other subjects as well. The rest were part-timers. Most of these part-timers were my students, usually poor boys and girls who knew almost no English and could not write a simple sentence.

Long and narrow, with one hundred and fifty students clustered on benches, my classroom was at the front of the building. Tractor trailers loaded with weapons from the Soviet Union or consumer goods from China thundered by at two-minute intervals. Teaching was impossible while a truck passed. Eventually I obtained a microphone. Unfortunately it was stuck together more with hope than tape and was usually broken. When it was repaired, either I couldn't use it because of static in the system or the electricity was off. As a result, I lectured by cupping my hands in front of my mouth and shouting. Throat sprays and pills quickly became more necessary to my teaching than paper and pencils.

The students themselves were a diverse group of boys and girls—rich and poor, religious and nonreligious, young and old. For many it was the first time they had attended class with members of the opposite sex. English was extremely popular; French was taught, but only fifty or sixty students each year majored in French in comparison to the three hundred and fifty or four hundred who majored in English. Enrollment numbers were never exact; faculty members never received a roll, and the president himself was not sure how many students were in the university.

My students dreamed of going to America. Despite Syria's close military ties with the Soviet Union, Russian was not taught because students refused to study it. If language is the greatest propaganda instrument in the world, then the West has won massive propaganda victories in the Middle East. Indeed America's cultural hegemony over Syria is amazing. Although our trade with Syria is not large, and ignorance of America is widespread, Syrians equate American with modernity and opportunity. Many students had cousins in the United States and studied English in hopes that it would provide the key which would magically open doors to America and golden treasures. "Go to America," a boy told me, "and shine shoes. Return to Syria a merchant." Recently I received a letter from a student who had been raised in a small mountain village. He does not know where America is but he wants to come here.

This past summer he went for a day-long trip in the Mediterranean. The man who took him told him that they were near America. "I have acquainted on somebody from Saudane," the boy wrote; "he took me in a sojourn with him in the sea. We were about to reach AMERICA. I asserted him to do so but he didn't do it. He was always in a hurry and for this I hated him."

Countries in transition from an agricultural to a mixed economy often overvalue modernity and suffer from what in effect are cultural inferiority complexes. In Syria even those who hope that the resurgence of Islam will enable them to retain some traditional mores recognize that the forces of modernization are practically impossible to oppose successfully. "The eastern," a conservative Moslem girl wrote, "now are hanging by the western's tail. The westerns have the progression in working, living, eating, but the easterns haven't. The westerns have also the dissoulution. And by the time we will have it so." Syrian secondary schools drum in the "dissoulution": the failings of America and capitalism. Occasionally attacks on capitalism cropped up in student essays. "The capitalist people," a boy wrote, "believe in all kinds of stealing in order to ern much money. They built their happiness on other's misery. Money made them unhuman creatures as if they live in a forest." For most students such attacks did not take. Capitalism like socialism was a word used in politics rather than life. The vast majority of students wanted wealth and their own businesses. In developing countries in which tribal and traditional ties are being shattered, money confers both dignity and identity. Much is made, however, of our racial problems. On several occasions—and this must appear somewhere in a secondary school textbook—students asked me if it were true that a black man had to bow down whenever he met a white man on the street. Questions about race, though, seemed to come more from curiosity than belief in racial equality. Students greeted interracial marriage with disgust, and blacks, I was told, had smaller brains than whites. Students had little knowledge of American government or politics, though one boy did predict that Ronald Reagan would not be elected president because "he will be 70 after erection."

The abilities of first-year students varied, but at the beginning of the year most were at a third or fourth grade level in English. They could not speak or write a sentence, and in first-term composition I taught primarily simple and compound sentences. During the second term I made students write three- to five-hundred-word essays, and I read and marked more than eighteen hundred of these. Much improvement was made, but I am certain that this coming year the deluge of rote learning will wash away all their experience in my classes.

The students were my joy. We had no adult friends aside from our landlord and his wife, neither of whom spoke English; the French couple; occasional American visitors from Damascus; and one teacher who lived an hour and a half away. The faculty at Tishreen was not sophisticated enough to realize that the only Americans in Latakia were just a teacher and his wife. Two members of the faculty told us they had been warned to avoid us because we might work for the CIA. When the Cultural Affairs Officer from the embassy delivered our air freight, he visited the assistant dean. As soon as he left, the dean asked me if he was a spy. From that date in early October until mid-February, the assistant dean avoided me and we did not speak.

I soon had a huge following among the students and, like a bitch in heat, was not always sure I enjoyed it. After classes every day, students walked uptown with me to talk and practice their English. In the mornings they waited to catch me on the way to the university. My wife and I rarely went shopping without running into students. During the break between terms we went to Jordan and Egypt. Unable to find us, students left notes at the stores we frequented. When we returned in February, a bookseller gave me the following letter: "I havn't ability to express about my feelings. is it correct that a man need to see his brother again? if you have, or if you would like. When you catch this letter, said to my friend, who is the owner of library. when I can see you Because I need to see you. I am eager to see you. Your effectionate friend."

Many students invited us to their villages, and the days we spent visiting were the happiest and also the most tiring—because no one spoke English well—that we spent in Syria. At the beginning of the year when they could not speak English, students communicated by notes which they labored over like sculptors. A girl who had worked on her simple sentences invited us to her village, writing "I live in a Beutiful town. It is called Jable. I want you to visit it with your waif. In jable my family will BE happy when you and your waif visits us. my mother also want me to calld us. Then if you came Y feel too happy. I writ theses composition Becaus Y respect you. And Y admir very much of your waif. It is a gentil and Beautiful woman. what you said, yes, or no. A simple sentences."

Early in the year a teacher warned me that professors did not talk to students outside the classroom or office. I paid no attention to the warning and must have been a dis-

turbing influence. Vague cultural assumptions support the
Fulbright scholar program. Generally it is assumed that
academic exchanges build bridges between peoples and
cultures and, in the case of American grantees, broaden
their horizons. What the Council for International Exchange
of Scholars does not say, but what the State Department
correctly assumes, is that the Fulbright program is a propaganda effort. In Syria the State Department seems interested in establishing links with, and presenting a favor-
able picture of America to the people who have or will
have influence. Emphasis is not on the masses but on the
elite, and with Syrian-American relations at an ebb, the
cultural branch of the embassy avoids disturbing the sen-
sibilities of those who have power. In contrast, the Fulbright
program, as it developed in my case, was educationally
revolutionary. American simplicity and democracy go
counter to the Syrian educational system. By encouraging
class discussion and original thought, and by treating the
students seriously, I implicitly criticized the methods of
other professors. Fresh educational air is not necessarily
pleasant educational air, and instead of attracting the educational elites, I put them off. Although the nation is osten-
sibly socialist, people in Syria are not equal. Money and
position shape castes, and tribal, village, and religious ties
often determine success in the university and outside it. At
the end of the first term, the assistant dean lost his post.
The ways of Syrian university politics are complex but I
was told the student association had complained repeatedly
that he was arrogant. During the second term, the man cultivated student leaders. Outside the cafeteria was a battered
Ping-Pong table. One day the former dean appeared with a
pair of sneakers. He put them in his desk and wore them

when he played table tennis with students. Dignity mattered a great deal to him; associating with students was bad enough but wearing porter's shoes must have been hateful. What he thought about me, my shoes, and my easy ways, I shudder to think. As propaganda I think my year was successful, but not in the way it was intended to be. Since returning to the United States I have received many letters from students. These students are comparatively poor and will never become cabinet ministers or Ph.D.'s, but will instead be housewives and village schoolmasters. None will ever be singled out for cultivation by our State Department. Instead of building cultural bridges with the people who politically or educationally matter in the Third World, perhaps the Fulbright program undermines such constructions.

Syria exhausted me emotionally. Syrian students, with their society in transition from a conservative rural Moslem culture to a modified urban western culture, face confusing problems. Rarely do they express their confusion or frustration publicly because they believe it will be interpreted as political disenchantment and they themselves will disappear. In private, they ask for personal advice and voice their disgust with the state of the nation. Private revenge, although discouraged by sophisticated urbanites, still exists in villages. One boy, for example, after recounting a harsh tale to me, asked if I thought he should kill the villain of the piece. Some people in his village thought he should, he said, but he wondered what a Westerner would do.

For women, western feminist concerns about equal job opportunity are beside the point. In Syria women are not equal to men. The birth of a girl is often an occasion for unhappiness rather than celebration. "I was the second girl in my family," a student wrote; "my father went out for three days when I was born in spite of he already had a son." Because I was the representative of a progressive society, students frequently believed that I could solve problems which involved a conflict between conservative family or community traditions and modern individualism. Traditionally, a girl's father chose her husband for her. "But the great wish is to meet my love and to live with him forever," a girl wrote in an essay; "I pray for him. And I implore God to gather us one day. I Love person sinc when my age was six years . . . Each of can't live without the other. But the great problem is my family. They did not agree to marry him . . . and there is another problem takes place now. A lawer came to my hous. And he became friend of my family. He want to engage me. All my family agree with him. But I refuse. Because I want to marry my childhood friend whom I love. I hate that Lawer. I wish I did not see him. But he always comes to our house. This is my problem. So I ask professor pickering to advice me. But not at the class. And God bless you."

Amid what would be considered harsh repression from a western feminist point of view was a great deal of joy. The girls in my classes forever gathered in the hall and giggled and laughed. When I assigned telling a typical Syrian story as an essay topic, many more girls than boys turned in broadly funny tales. "In Lattakia," one wrote, "when women meet other's they began to talk and talk in many speech and sometimes they tells special jokes like: Once two old wife and husband wanted to ceremony at their eighty marriage feast. The old woman wore her Soiree dress, then they brought the great dinnar to made their party more beautiful. The old woman bent to put the soup for her husband her pap loll out of her dress and they nearly touched the vessel of the soup. The old man said: I want the soup without meat."

Until they came to know me, I was a cartoon figure to many students. Their perception of me, like the Third World's perception of America and Americans, had in great part been shaped by television advertising, pop music, and B-grade films. If Westerners are not thought immoral, they are certainly believed to be enlightened, and this led to embarrassing moments. Having received many invitations, I suspected nothing when a female student invited me to a cake party after class one Thursday in the school cafeteria. When Thursday afternoon arrived, the girl told me that the authorities would not let her have the party at school; consequently, she had changed its location to her apartment and said her cousin would drive us there. A white Mercedes picked us up at the front gate. As we roared through Latakia at what seemed fifty miles an hour, the girl added that none of her friends had been able to come to the party, and she hoped I would understand. Perspiration and understanding broke out simultaneously. Resembling a set from an Egyptian film, the apartment was furnished in "Louis Farouk," gaudy and expensive gold and silver. Between two sofas in the living room was a low table. On it were several kinds of luncheon meats, trays of nuts, assorted cheeses, oranges, apples, lemons, chocolates, two types of imported beer, a bottle of Johnnie Walker, two bowls of pink and white carnations, and a three-layered cake covered with whipped cream. When I sat on a couch, the girl sat next to me. The cousin started to sit opposite, but then he looked at his watch, said he had an important appointment, apologized, and left.

When I am nervous, I talk. For an hour I talked incessantly while the girl stared into my eyes. When I slowly slid to the end of the couch, she followed, serving me cake and urging me to drink. When half my backside hung over the edge of the couch and I was in danger of falling on the floor and undergoing I knew not what, I stood up and asked to see the apartment. Politely I complimented the bathroom; my hostess responded by turning on the water and asking if I would like a bath. An imitation tiger-skin blanket covered the double bed in the bedroom. If ever I wanted, she said, I could spend the night there. This was Arab hospitality carried to an extreme. Finally, after I had inspected all the rooms, I felt unable to face the couch again. I thanked my hostess and cut and ran—not, however, without presents for my wife: the carnations and the remains of the cake.

Although it may seem obvious, I was never certain what the girl wanted. Rich and living alone—something unique among the students—I suspect she may have fallen prey to the cinematic depiction of Westerners. Maybe she simply wanted a high grade. Perhaps, however, this was an attempt to compromise me. As the only Americans in Latakia, my wife and I suffered from paranoia. People stared at us wherever we went and we could not fade into a crowd. By December we began to think we were watched. Our mail had been routinely opened; often letters did not arrive, and occasionally odd things happened. When my wife's parents opened one of her letters, they found a snapshot inside. They assumed it was our landlord's family. It wasn't; the people were strangers. The person reading the mail prob-

ably had several letters open on his desk, and when he re-
sealed them he mistakenly put the picture into my wife's
letter.

According to rumor, there were nineteen secret police
organizations in Syria. I knew of five in Latakia, two having
their local headquarters on streets immediately behind our
apartment building. In the spring, an acquaintance who had
a friend in one branch of the secret police obtained copies
of reports on me. In all university classes there were spies—
students paid to report on professors to branches of the
secret police. Although this process did not bother me, because I was a foreigner and able to leave the country, it
frightened and inhibited Syrian teachers. Only one aspect
of the reports about me was interesting. It was alleged that
I favored girls in my classes. Supposedly I cultivated their
friendship, not for "sexual relations," but because I wanted
to discuss politics with them. While at the "party" in the
girl's apartment, I had asked her many questions about the
problems in Latakia in order to keep us talking. Showing
little interest in sex, I must have shown an immoderate concern about politics. Perhaps she was the source of the reports. Most probably she was not, but it is rather nice to
think she might have been.

A student whose parents forced her to attend university
wrote an essay in which she described her dislike of studying. "I always," she wrote, "asked our God to rest me from
this calamity. I want to sleep without any think of the
studies." This Fulbright lecturer seldom thought of studies.
Grading compositions at home took much time, but class
preparations were minimal. Day after day I repeated les-
sons in composition, trying to teach my students basic
grammar rules. In prose I taught *The Old Man and the Sea*

and the first forty pages of George Orwell's *Coming Up for Air*, this latter being a terrible choice for first-year students whose reading was frequently at the primer level. In composition I spent most of my time explaining idioms and defining simple words like green or blue, living room or dining room. Rarely was I able to venture very far into thematic topics; when I did, two-thirds of the class was lost. Similarly, my colleagues and I never discussed literature. The university and Syria itself did not provide the kind of atmosphere in which such thought could flourish. Good books in English could not be bought in Latakia, and since I was not an Arabist the possibility of research did not exist. Consequently every night I went to sleep as my student wished, "without any think of the studies."

For the Fulbrighter in Syria and perhaps in the Third World in general, what happens outside class influences the academic experience more than what happens in class. During the first weeks, thoughts abdominal replace thoughts intellectual; the anatomy changes and one becomes more bowel and less brain. Once things internal are acclimated, however, then external events and conditions determine the quality of the experience. Although my wife and I saw much of Syria, and although many nights in Latakia were filled with the sound of music—the *1812 Overture* with mortar and kalishnikov effects—we were usually bored. The cinemas showed either broad Egyptian comedies or gory Italian and American gangster films. There was only one good restaurant in town, and it was frequently closed because of the troubles. To survive we bought a radio, listened to the BBC's Middle East service, and planned vacations. We had a television set, and once a week saw "The Virginian." Sometimes "Switch" appeared. Those were evenings to be savored. In general Syrian television was a dreary patriotic affair. Throughout the year party functionaries opened power plants and Assad accepted flowers from masses of cheering school children. The patriotic drumbeat never stopped, and on the evening news, the words *America, Israel, Zionism,* and *Camp David* were intoned like a litany as the government blamed the country's troubles on external enemies. Few people took the propaganda seriously. According to a shopkeeper in Latakia, the mayor called the merchants together in order to explain why there was inflation and trade was poor. Camp David was behind everything, the mayor explained. When the mayor finished speaking, a merchant stood up in the back of the room and said, "You are mayor. When Camp David came to Latakia, why didn't you order the police to arrest him and put him on a bus to another city?"

When the Iranians first took the embassy personnel in Tehran hostage, and the State Department conducted a token evacuation of Americans from eleven Moslem countries, our feelings of isolation and vulnerability grew. We were out on a limb far from Damascus and communication was difficult. Our landlord had a telephone, but the link between Latakia and Damascus was often disrupted. In class, students who were nervous because I might leave Syria assured me that my wife and I had nothing to fear. "We Moslems love you," students said, and promised to take us to their villages if danger developed. One acquaintance, whose brother-in-law was a general, declared he would transport us to his village in a tank if necessary. The first time I heard such things, they made me more comfortable. But after I had been reassured some forty times, nagging worries and feelings of vulnerability began to grow. Where there was so much smoke, or concern, there must be a little flame.

The only member of the English department whom I considered a friend indirectly fanned our worries. A Syrian and a brilliant student, he had completed his Ph.D. in Britain, published essays in good academic journals, and returned to Syria to teach. Apolitical and perhaps the most honest man I have ever met—and in Syria to be completely honest is practically impossible, and even dangerous—he suffered from the accidental disability of being an Alawite. He had taught at the University of Damascus but had left, among other reasons, because he feared for his life. Now as assassinations spread to Latakia—two streets behind our apartment a man was murdered—my friend became convinced that an attempt would be made on his life. Although he lived an hour and a half from Latakia, he spent two nights a week in the city. In the afternoons he would visit and confide his fears to us. His was the only literate conversation we enjoyed in English, but since his fears were all-consuming, our subject matter was limited. In our isolation—feeling under siege because of Iran, hearing America violently attacked on television as President Assad tried to blame Syria's internal troubles on external forces, and talking with our friend about little except his fears—we began to get the wind up. With no one to help us put our foolish anxieties into reasonable perspective, we retreated more into our apartment and marked off on the calendar the days until term break. Eventually, the embassy called us to Damascus to inform us about the state of affairs in Syria and Iran and to reassure us, but it is in the nature of a diplomat's existence, in Syria at least, that form and circumstance separate him from what is happening in the country. He reads scores of informative reports and dines with important people, but these are no substitute for being able to move about freely. Knowing that we felt isolated, the ambassador suggested that we move to the University of Damascus or the University of Aleppo. Aleppo, he said, was a particularly appealing city. Because I felt responsible for my students at Tishreen and because of a perhaps adolescent dislike of appearing a quitter, we remained in Latakia. This was fortunate; two months later disturbances shattered Aleppo's appeal, and the university, to all intents and purposes, closed for the year.

Like scholars, diplomats depend upon sources for their knowledge. Aside from us, the embassy had no sources in Latakia or at least what they had been told about the city was inaccurate. After we returned, the embassy's assurances, which had sounded so good in Damascus, evaporated like rain on a hot sidewalk. On those days which my frightened colleague spent in Latakia he went to the university by different means and different ways. By mid-December I too varied my route to the university. The end of term brought great relief. Almost immediately my wife and I left for a month in Jordan and Egypt, where we would not stand out but would be just two more nondescript Westerners. There we could escape the shackling authentic experience and enjoy the comfortable tourist experience.

We returned to Latakia in late January, relaxed and ready for whatever came our way. I graded five hundred exams, and when classes began ten days late, on February 19, I was eager to start. I was also pleased because I had demanded and gotten a second-year course: Shakespeare. The chairman, a man with vast resources of cunning, invited us to his home for tea and urged me to teach nineteen hours—prose, composition, and Shakespeare. I had learned my lesson the first term and was not accommodating; composition and Shakespeare were enough. Once classes started, the term quickly became chaotic.

Although Syria suffers from a dearth of trained teachers, no exemptions—legal ones—are made for military service. University professors must serve like everyone else. Frequently, this is done after they finish their graduate education and are teaching at a university. Usually after they complete their basic training, they are seconded back to the university where they teach as second lieutenants, distinguishable from civilians only in that they receive military pay instead of the much higher university pay. Basic training begins in the fall and spring, not in the summer, so that universities are often left with half-taught courses on their hands. In March my friend who had been frightened for his life left the university to begin his military training. At the same time, the chairman, who was also liable for military service, came down with an attack of diabetes and disappeared to Damascus for two or three weeks. In April one of our two demonstrators left Syria on an AID fellowship to work for his Ph.D. in the United States. The only persons left to teach courses were the assistant dean (recently demoted to an ordinary teacher), the second demonstrator, and I. Courses were piled on the demonstrator, and the assistant dean's wife taught part-time. The department muddled through the term. Many courses, however, went untaught for long periods and the students suffered.

Even more inhibiting to the students' progress than the absence of professors was the state of the nation. In February violence in Syria grew geometrically. By the end of the month Aleppo was a little Beirut, and the Fulbright lecturer at Aleppo University had left the country. Latakia was not so violent. Assassinations occasionally occurred in the daytime, but most trouble happened at night. Dynamite bombs exploded practically every evening. Counting them became exciting and addictive; in May, when a temporary calm descended, life seemed less intense and we were bored. Because they did not want to be on the streets at dusk, students avoided classes that met after four o'clock. My colleagues received notes and telephone calls threatening their lives. My teaching timetable changed radically. No one consulted me; I learned about the changes only when I went to class at the wrong time. Eventually a reason for the changing timetable became apparent as my morning classes became afternoon classes. A foreigner was safer on the streets late in the afternoon than was a Syrian professor. Guards armed with tommy guns had guarded the faculty of letters twenty-four hours a day throughout the year. Now there were more guards. And on some days when there had been much trouble the night before, guards seemed to outnumber students.

Gun battles began to occur at night between the Moslem Brothers and their sympathizers and the secret police. In Aleppo and elsewhere, Russians were murdered. This caused us some worry because many Latakians who had never seen Americans assumed we were Russians. People often said "Russians" in a derogatory tone when we passed them on the street. "My God, sir, my God," a nervous girl burst out in class, "you look so like a Russian." Acquaintances became worried, and one of them took matters into his own hands. Meeting us in town, he informed us he had done us a favor. He said he had discovered that many people thought we were Russians. To prevent a mistake, he said, he had spread the word to people who in turn would inform those behind the violence that we were not Russians but Americans. For such a favor I was not grateful. Nobody gets things right in Syria; it is better for one to lie low and say nothing than to have attention called to one.

The troubles came to a head in March. Elite commandos appeared in Latakia, and together with the secret police they attempted to crush the terrorists. From the balcony of our apartment I watched gun battles. For two weeks life in the university slowed almost to a halt. Students stayed away from class. Out of one hundred and fifty students in a class, two or three who lived nearby might show up. Walking to school was nerve-wracking yet intoxicating. From behind sandbags, soldiers guarded street corners; often streets were completely empty or sealed off. In its disregard for truth, rumor waxed poetic. Although the violence subsided—it never died out—classes did not return to normal. It would have been abnormal if they had. Alawite students from the villages were frightened and in some cases embittered. Sunnis became more opposed to the government while Christians damning both sects withdrew into their own community. The only assurance that the future seemed to hold was that someday there would be more and worse violence.

During the period of the worst troubles, I taught *Hamlet* to those members of my second-year class who attended. The parallels between Hamlet's rotten Denmark and Assad's Syria were marked. Corruption from the head of state infected the nation. Many of the people resembled Hamlets or Rosencrantzes and Guildensterns. Either, like Hamlet, they found their world and responsibilities bewildering, or like Rosencrantz and Guildenstern they were little spokes joined to a big wheel which if it broke would destroy them.

Obliquely I drew comparisons between Denmark and Syria. Some understood and were knowingly silent; others studiously and carefully avoided understanding. The majority were not linguistically good enough to move beyond language to theme. If, however, most of my students did not see, or refused to acknowledge, the contemporary significance of *Hamlet*, I could not avoid it. During the first term I faced no important academic questions. Although I was teaching at a lower level than I had taught before, I knew that what I was doing was useful. English was the language of science, medicine, business, and diplomacy. Like a technician I was teaching a skill my students could use. In contrast, *Hamlet* forced me to confront the relevancy of literature to one's spiritual or moral life, a subject which I had always avoided in the United States because it seemed beside the point. Was my teaching *Hamlet*, which universalized and indirectly examined the problems Syrians faced, one of the most meaningful things I had ever done in a classroom? Or was teaching literature and discussing Hamlet's inaction while people were dying on the streets one of the most meaningless things I ever did? I never decided.

Throughout the turmoil, my relationship with the students was constant. On Easter I received several cards. My Moslem students knew that it was an occasion for a Christian feast, but most were not sure which one. One card read, "Merry Christmas to My Sincerely Teacher." When my wife became ill in late April, eight Moslem girls, all wrapped in scarves and long coats, came to our apartment with armfuls of flowers. On the last day of class, students asked me to autograph their books. There were tears, reluctant farewells, and assertions of lasting friendship. The year had been difficult; I made almost no adult friends. I had done no research. The seven hundred examinations I graded in July convinced me that three-quarters of my students would never complete their studies and the bright dreams and hopes they shared with me would wither. No Fulbright lecturer would follow me to Latakia the next year and most of what I had accomplished with even my best students would be swiftly erased.

I went to Syria when my professional career seemed at a crossroads. A university press had accepted my second book. My articles appeared in the better literary quarterlies, and journals were beginning to write me soliciting essays. When I was in Syria, my professional work had to be shunted aside; unseized opportunities passed on to other people. Was the year worth it? I am not sure, but when I left, a student presented a poem she had written to me. Although it was embarrassingly fulsome, its sentiment touched me and almost made me glad I had spent the year in Syria. "Like the effect of sunset," she wrote, "Like the gone of the moon, / Like shadwos spreading in space, / Like storms which destroy everything / Like all these things your leaving will be. / Your leaving will fill our hearts with sadness and dullness. / Your leaving will take the dynamic thing from our life. / Maybe my words is very big for the situation, / But that is really what I feel and the truth. / So you have the right by getting back home again, / But we havn't the right to possess whom we loved. / God bless you, our wonderful teacher. / God help you with your coming life. / God take care of you and your wife fore ever. / I want of you just to remember that there are / Students loves you and think of you forever."

A Thousand and One Classrooms

Mickey rode out of Groton like the Marlboro Man, in boots, a ten-gallon hat, and carrying a bull shooter. He disappeared after the first class, and I didn't see him again until I decided to treat myself to a bottle of wine. While bending over looking at a cheap chablis, I felt an arm curl cousin-like around my shoulder. It was Mickey with a quart of Jim Beam in one hand and now me under the other. "Sam," he said, "I want to congratulate you on that lecture. Never have I heard a first-year man do so well. You might have noticed," he continued without a pause, "that I have not been in class recently. I'm a senior and have," he added with an intimate squeeze, "certain responsibilities. You probably won't see much of me." Before I could straighten, much less answer, he moved his hand from my shoulder to just above my elbow and leading me down the aisle, he pointed confidentially to a beaujolais. "Sam," he said, "I recommend this." Then balling his hand into a fist and shaking it like a coach encouraging a nervous substitute, he added, "Keep up the good work, sport." With that he strode out of the door and into the night. That was the last I saw of Mickey. I gave him a *D*. The wine he recommended wasn't worth a damn.

Mickey deserved a higher grade. He and others like him have given me many *A* times since I began teaching. By treating education cavalierly such students deflate academic pretension and lighten teachers' lives. When I taught in

Jordan four students once handed in the same essay. I called Hashem into my office and asked him where he got the essay. "Allah gave it to me," he answered. "There must be a mimeograph machine in heaven then," I said leaning forward angrily, "because three other students turned in the same essay." Hashem paused, folded his hands together in his lap, and rolled his eyes toward the ceiling before he replied. "Ah, sir," he said, "there are many true believers in the class. Allah is merciful and compassionate and would not forget them."

Hashem and his friends passed. Teachers cannot resist tricksters because they themselves are snake-oil salesmen preaching the miraculous virtues of their cure-alls to students and congressmen. Manner, not matter, is important. I learned this long ago while I was a graduate assistant at Princeton. One Saturday afternoon while Brown was skinning the Princeton tiger, my friends and I inhaled whiskey sours. Since the game was lost and our thermoses empty, we started home at halftime. As I tottered toward the ramp to leave the stadium, there was great turmoil above me. I looked up and saw Benjamin, my best student, pointing at me, laughing, and yelling. My career, I thought, was over before it began. If Benjamin could see from that far away that I was uncorked, others would have noticed. I didn't look forward to class on Monday. When Benjamin came into the room, he glanced at me and then turned red. He whispered something to the boy next to him. Involuntarily the boy's hand rose to his mouth in horror. "Should I resign now or later," I thought. After class Benjamin approached me. "Mr. Pickering," he said, "I want to apologize. I had too much to drink on Saturday at the football game. You are my favorite teacher," he continued, his voice husky with emotion; "when I saw you, I felt happy and wanted to say hello. Instead I behaved miserably." "Ben," I said wrapping my arm around his shoulders, "Ben, I knew you had too much to drink. Once, a long while ago, I did the same thing." "Oh, sir," he exclaimed. "No, enough, Ben," I continued taking him by the elbow and leading him to the door; "let bygones be bygones. Just don't let it happen again." Yes, yes indeed, Allah is merciful.

A lifetime of little duties shackles the university professor. Nothing he does is of much consequence. Teaching is the only profession I know in which one has the same responsibilities at forty-five, fifty-five, and seventy that he had at thirty. While his peers regulate the corporate interests of the nation, the professor spends days in prolonged discussions of inessentials, whether or not, for example, freshman English should require eight essays or six essays and two examinations. At forty he sees college compatriots he thought less talented assume positions of power and become men not simply of influence but of vision, grace, and understanding. Progressive responsibilities have challenged their abilities and led to growth while the professor's talents have atrophied. Like King Shahriyar in the *Arabian Nights* who loses faith in his wife then in all mankind, the teacher becomes despondent. Instead of chopping the heads off a succession of brides as did the King, the teacher decapitates ideas. He sinks into rumpled arrogance and like any member of a comfortable but ultimately impotent and listless class, he becomes a scoffer, damning change and originality.

Happily a remedy lies at hand. As Scheherazade's tales delivered the King from his melancholy, enabling him to imagine the beauty of life, so hours in the classroom can free the teacher from dryness of spirit and can stretch for a thousand and one days peopling eternity with Mickeys, Hashems and Benjamins. Enchantments stranger than those that bind genii influence students. When discussion in a writing course plodded through a ponderous account of post-adolescent love, Joe jumped out of his seat and holding up a two-by-three-foot picture of a rooster shouted, "What are we going to do about this chicken?" Before I could cook up a witty culinary retort, the boy next to him grabbed his shirt and said, "Hey man, you're going to get your stones crushed." Joe, who was flying on something stronger than the wings of a Rhode Island Red, answered, "I'm too high to get my stones crushed." "Man," the other boy replied, "they've got rock quarries even on the tops of mountains." Writing classes, of course, bring out the bewitched: the boy who brought a glass of orange juice to class, drank the juice, and then ate the glass or the girl who came with a cockatoo on her head and didn't say a word although the bird tried to speak.

One of my favorite stories in the *Arabian Nights* is "The Historic Fart." Although they are rarely historic, such things occur in the halls of ivy. Harold was the janitor who cleaned the English department where I once taught. He was a man addicted to high spirits and low living. While cleaning, particularly on Mondays, he would let fly rousers. This particular Monday Jonathan had come into my office to complain about a grade. Jonathan's conceptions were immaculate but his papers were flawed. I once attempted to cushion the inevitable *C* by praising the first sentence of an essay. "This sentence," I said, "is quite good." "It ought to be," Jonathan responded, "I wrote it." Jonathan was just biting into his complaint and my spirits when Harold went whistling past the open door. "Surely," Jonathan said, "if you had thought at all when you read this paragraph, you . . ." He did not finish the sentence as disgust swept across his face. "Good Lord," he exclaimed and then shuddering, he jerked his paper off my desk and left the office. A moment later I knew the reason. In this case an ill wind boded well and Jonathan never bothered me again.

Getting students out of the office before unpleasantness occurs requires skill. One morning after an inspired Freudian lecture on "Sleeping Beauty" and "The Frog Prince," a ferocious student trailed me into my office. "Professor Pickering," she said, her eyes redder than those of witches; "I have never been in a class with so much sex." "What ho!" I said; "whereabouts—where was it? I missed it. Were you involved? Good Lord, a nice girl like you," I continued as I looked at my watch and headed for the door. "I am sorry I have an appointment," I added and before she could say another word I was down the hall, around the corner, and hiding in the men's room. Often the less said in an office the better.

The new teacher is usually conscientious and expects his students to be the same. When a boy came to my office to reschedule a test being given the next hour, I turned on him like a roundhead and demanded an excuse. "I have to go home," Buck explained. "So do I—at one o'clock for lunch," I snapped, "why do you have to go home now?" I should have left well enough alone. Buck pointed downward. "Why are you pointing at the floor," I asked. "It's not the floor; I'm not pointing at the floor. I'm pointing at my . . ." and then he paused. "Lice, sir," he continued; "I have pubic lice." "Go!" I shouted waving my arm toward the door; "Go immediately and don't come back until they are gone. You need not see me about the exam. I will give a copy to the secretary and you can get it from her when you return." He went and I left shortly thereafter myself, stopping only to ask Harold to pay particular attention to the furniture when he cleaned my office. Since then no student has ever had to explain why he wanted to delay my examination.

The good educational life requires more tolerance than the good Christian life. In the good classroom many are chosen and both the path and gate are wide. It is easy to be a petty tyrant, mocking those that appear stupid, lazy, or weak. For six weeks Butch did not say a word in freshman English. Then one day when we were starting *King Lear*, I asked, "What do Goneril and Regan think about their father?" Amazingly Butch waved his hand. "Yes, Butch," I said with my sweetest honeysuckle smile. "They don't give a shit about their father," he replied. Like an unwed mother at an Episcopal Church, the answer made people roll their eyes and shift in their seats.

"No one," I thought, "can say that in my class" and I was tempted to be harsh. I wasn't; instead I answered, "absolutely right, they don't give a poop about their father." The absurdity of *poop* shifted attention from Butch to me. After class I called the dean of freshmen. I learned that Butch was a veteran who had spent thirteen months in hospitals and had been released only two weeks before school began. The dean was worried because he was silent in class. His speaking was a breakthrough both for him and for me as I learned that tolerance and kindness were more important than dignity.

Ideas are relatively unimportant in an English course. Occasionally a professor introduces a student to a subject that will influence his life but for the most part students carry the characters of teachers away in their memories and not ideas. When I received a *B* in a course at Sewanee, I went to Mr. Martin's office. "Mr. Martin," I said; "I made *A*'s on all the tests and yet I got a *B*. How can that be?" "Just a minute, poor Pickering," he said and rummaged through a file box. He pulled out a card and showed it to me. "Pickering, here are the mid-term grades from all your other courses. You had *B*'s; you are not an *A* student." "But Mr. Martin," I answered; "I got *A*'s in all those courses for the semester." "Pickering," he said looking at me over his glasses; "you are not lying are you." "No sir," I replied. "Oh, dear," he said picking up a pencil and writing a note; "I have made a mistake. Take this to the registrar." I got my *A* with little trouble; the registrar had seen many notes like mine.

When I was in college the relationship between faculty and students was less sane and more humane than now. Most English teachers came from small towns in which personalities were more important than ideas. As conversation concentrated on the comparatively static relationships in the town and rarely drifted to the abstract so literary criticism was historical, exploring the roots of what everybody agreed was a familiar tradition. Today English teachers come from cities. Town and tradition have almost vanished. In the city the phenomenon of movement rather than the influence of place or tradition is important. From traffic to neighborhoods all moves and one doesn't hear stories so much as he notices juxtapositions. The absurd abuts the rational and as landscapes and neighbors change rapidly, the only reality seems the abstract reality of ideas, not a narrative reality with a beginning, middle and end. From the city comes the contemporary critic who denies not simply literary tradition but texts themselves. In class the familiar relationship between student and teacher has gone the way of small town gossip and critics concentrate on the flow of ideas between people rather than on people themselves.

In a profession which pays lip and sometimes financial service to writing, putting literary criticism into perspective before one tumbles into uncritical despair is difficult. Chair fever strikes the professor early in his career. In graduate school students learn to admire authorities on Meredith or Clough and the brightest determine to occupy a chair some day, little imagining that it will fold beneath them and leave them flat with hearts aching and spirits broken. Immunization is not easily come by. Unknowingly a student vaccinated me. After returning to the United States after teaching a year in Jordan, I wrote Joseph, one of my former students, and mentioned I was writing a book. "How happy I was," he answered, "and still to receive a letter from you. I read it thrice, or more, enjoying your words as if you were present and talking with me. Through your words and lines, I draw a very beautiful picture of your face. I am happy to know," he continued, "that you are writing some books. I wish for you a very bright future in writings. I hope that you will be as prominent as Shakespeare one day."

Joseph's letter purged me and dreams of Harvard and a chair disappeared before they became incurable. Not only do letters from students cure academic pretension but they bring joy. "Dear prophessor," Mayada wrote from Syria, "Your nice letter just arrived. I read it deeply. It made me like the bird in the sky. Since I receive it, my pleasure seem to be finding no place on the earth." When melancholy falls upon teachers, they often turn to colleagues for relief. Unlike Mayada's bird soaring aloft on pleasure, wordly wisdom has clipped their wings. What colleagues say is frequently memorable but it rarely points to pleasure beyond the earth. "I hope I never see the day," a teacher told me, "when the son of a millionaire can't get into Dartmouth." A colleague in the Mideast belonged to one of the richest families in the nation. While many students lived in hovels in refugee camps, she lived like a princess. "What I dislike so much about the poor," she once told me, "is their envy."

"Your students won't resent it," a colleague confided in me, "if you give them *A*'s." The world still lies open and promising before students and unlike adults they don't resent much. Few students believe they will fail in life and their bright optimism is catching. The lives of students like Scheherazade's stories breathe life into the brittle academic day. Although Pixie had a smile like Christmas in the country, she spent an unhappy first term in college. Her parents telephoned almost every night to see if she were in her room. In the dormitory, Pixie's nicest intentions turned sour. When she cooked fudge for her floor, she left out the sugar. Aside from giving her a copy of *The Joy of Cooking*, I could do little about the fudge. But I did manage to sweeten her parents on Parents' Weekend. They came to my home for sherry and as we chatted, I said, "Pixie seems unhappy. When such a nice girl is unhappy, something is wrong with the world." The telephone calls stopped, and one bright spring morning as I walked across the college green, I heard a girl cry out, "Professor Pickering! Professor Pickering!" Pixie came running across the grass. "Professor," she burst out when she reached me; "the most wonderful thing has happened. I think I'm in love." So was I but Pixie never knew it.

It would take a saint not to fall in love with his students. And I am afraid that as Adam said when the angel found him strolling about in the garden in a blue blazer, Oxford grey trousers, and weejuns and with a cigar in one hand and a snifter in the other, "the young woman asked me and I did eat." Age brings, if not morality, at least incapacity, and climbing stairs, not youthful beauty, takes the breath away. Still it is harder for the not-so-young teacher to escape his youthful ways than for an anaconda to shed his skin.

Susan made Burns's rose look like a wallflower. This past year when I handed out a final examination, Susan stumbled against my desk. She was sick. Because it was eight o'clock Sunday morning and the lounges in the building were locked, I decided to take her to the infirmary, which, happily, was only four hundred yards away. Since Susan could hardly walk, I put my arm around her back and under her arm and set off half-carrying her. Every ten or so steps, she fell weakly against my chest and I had to put my other arm around her for support. Since it was early in the morning, I hoped that luck would be with me and no one would see us. Alas, age shortens luck. "Well," my chairman said later that morning, "what was she like?" "Who?" I answered suddenly wishing that I were in the infirmary. "The good-looking babe—who the hell else?" he said. "Sick," I blurted out, "she was sick and I took her to the infirmary." "Any jackass looking at you two could see that you took her," he said, "just try to do it in a less public place in the future."

A term resembles a life in miniature. The beginning with its turmoil and frenetic activity is birth and youth. The middle with its intense work and energy parallels man's active creative years while the end drifting to final examinations resembles old age and death. At the completion of a term students leave for their homes or begin new lives. Drained and alone, the teacher can become despondent. The next term brings rebirth but the trauma of beginning and ending, breaking life into four-month cycles, is exhausting. Moreover, the structure of the term forces the teacher into taking short views of life. Instead of focusing on long-range goals, dreams fall into the rhythm of the term and become associated with the immediate. Instead of being part of an indefinite and consequently infinitely shapeable future, failure and gratification, and the concomitant loss of possibilities, become the present. Teaching makes one acutely aware of loss. Not only do students vanish just when one gets to know them but the teacher confronts his mortality and deteriorating powers each term. Unlike other occupations in which one associates primarily with one's peers and with whom one ages imperceptibly and often unconsciously, the teacher faces perennial youth. Each fall the teacher is a year older while the students are the same age. A generation may pass but students are always twenty. To escape the sense of loss one has to escape self, and the best way is through the classroom which like Scheherazade's stories not only entertain but also teach. Loss of youth is only a trifle when compared to what students lose. When Ali missed a week of classes at the University of Jordan, he came to my office and apologized. He had been in Lebanon. Phalangists, he said, had overrun his village. They had killed twelve members of his family, seven men and five women. He was the oldest male left and had to arrange the burials. Shrugging his shoulders, he looked out the window for a moment, then turned to me and said, "Christians kill Moslems; Moslems kill Christians; that's life."

For teachers the thousand and one classrooms are life. If literature as some critics say is about itself, then certainly the classroom is about itself. My wife came from the classroom. Her father taught me in graduate school, and one fall when we were both in London on fellowships, I visited him and his family. As I went to the classroom for a job and stayed for life, so I went to his house for literature and stayed for a wife. At the conclusion of the *Arabian Nights,* King Shahriyar embraced Scheherazade and proclaimed a feast. The feast ended after thirty days. For the professor the feast never ends. What is cooked may not appeal to the gourmet but the courses are always intriguing. Sometimes the teacher himself is the main course. "I do say that I missed you rare fried," Ahmad wrote, "I am happy to hear that you want to write essay about Syria. I hope to be accompanied with well-known." The university prefers its professors hard-boiled and not "rare fried" and I will never be well-known. I will, though, be entertained and happy.

Occupational Hazard

Like the indiscretions of youth, some ailments are too boring to be bandied about in medical journals. While a thousand scalpels would leap from operating rooms to preserve the honor of cholera morbus, hardly a lancet would be raised in defence of tennis elbow or housewife's knee. Yet if such ailments do not inspire articles too profound for seriousness, a survey of academics from Maine to California would reveal that occupational hazards spare no named chair. In the paneled halls of ivy lurks pomposity.

Rarely fatal, the virus usually leads to a comfortable mental state in which the sufferer becomes inaccessible to thought. What the disease lacks in virulence, however, it makes up for in epidemic proportions. Even the brightest, blue-eyed, fit young instructor fresh from an exhilarating jog through graduate school eventually slows, swells, and sickens. No antidote has been found for the corrupting effects of being treated by undergraduates as one of the wise men of the ancient world. Slowly the belief that one is Delphic gets under the skin and becomes incurable.

But if medical science has found no vaccine for those sensations so warm to the ego, it has at least marked the stages of the disease's progress. Soon after his first book meets with friendly critical nods, the young assistant professor becomes susceptible. Giving the lie to the old adage that clothes make the man, the sufferer strides into pomposity's deceptive sartorial stage. Paunching slightly with confidence, he wraps himself in a tattered Afghan in the winter and lets his toes dangle through the slits of Rhodean sandals in the summer. When reversed his paisley tie delivers a full-fisted message, matched in its rough whimsicality only by the lavender shorts he wears to the President's tea party. To the outsider this would seem a young man on the way out. But to the cognoscenti, this is clearly a man on the way up. They know that it is only a short step from Afghan to Brooks Brothers. The paisley will be weeded out and Bronzini and Sulka will blossom in its place. The sandals will languish in the closet while those sweet harbingers of spring Whitehouse and Hardy wingtips will escort a new associate professor to that tenured land where Scotch and water purl against ice cubes like the Afton flowing gently to the sea.

Not long afterwards, our subject becomes "Guggenheimed" and flies away for a year in the British Library. A penchant for Gauloises and Harvey's amontillado and the appearance, much anticipated, of *the book* mark the disease's inexorable progress. After the return from Bloomsbury, Vanity Fair prints of willowy John Whistler and languid Lord Leighton decorate the sufferer's office walls while the poster celebrating the annual rattlesnake roundup in Sweetwater, Texas, curls in the wastecan. In the classroom a great vowel shift occurs as our not-so-young young man sounds like he lost his youth on the playing fields of Eton or under the shadow of King's College Chapel. On the title page of *the book*, L. Stafford Brown rises like the phoenix from the ashes of Leroy Brown, Jr.

Alas, university life is imperfect. Unlike the happy bovine, the graying academic cannot forever graze in green pastures blissfully ruminating over the cud of learning long digested. Before our sufferer answers the great cattle call from above and assumes the mantle of a named chair, he becomes aware of his illness. While perusing the shelves of the bookstore and pondering a list of books to be read during summer vacation, he hears a student confuse him with Balaam's inelegant long-eared beast of burden. At a colleague's Christmas party, he harangues the pert helpmate of a junior member of the department with learned jocularity. Certain he had left her in the living room like Saul on the road to Damascus blinded by light, he returns from the Necessary House in time to hear her compare him to that befeathered creature whose cackling saved Rome from the Gauls. Awareness sweeps down upon him and he vows to take a cure.

Unfortunately diagnosis is easier than treatment. Several remedies are available; and although each may cause a temporary remission, none can completely eradicate the disease. First our sufferer grows long sideburns and begins frequenting the society of the young and ignorant. With enthusiastic joie de vivre, he puts off the old and selects a new wife from his seminar on the Age of Reason. Sadly he discovers that ignorance charms only at a distance and youth like okra rises on the cultivated stomach. The days when he could burst from bed to greet the sun like a morning glory are over. Before the bottoms of his jogging shoes wear thin, his wife decamps. The shoes join the sandals in the back of the closet, and our professor places his hopes for a cure in canine informality. When the leaves turn gold above the autumn mists, our professor comes to the office carrying a large blanket and leading a small dog. Alas, as little acorns grow into big oaks, so small dogs grow into large beasts. By the summer all the days are dog-days. And when Kim suddenly develops heartworms, the professor openly weeps but privately mixes a decanter of martinis.

Our sufferer's Indian summer of heartiness is over. Elevated to the department chair, he ignores the petty world scrabbling below and nods into graying dignity. Pomposity brooks opposition no longer, and the professor becomes a wonderful old boy in whose presence ideas flap heavily and fall to the ground like dying swans. Alumni recall his incompetence fondly. And when asked to speak at their annual dinner, he charms away fret from their busy lives by stumbling about sleepily. In his presence hardened men of the world drain their cups and recall that splendid time when they were boyish "Sons of old Cayuga."

On the campus stories describing his terse "ah ha's" and thoughtful "um's" abound. His enrollments swell as gentlemanly B's are bestowed with grand largesse. While students dream of girls as sugary as peppermint, the old boy puffs his pipe, rolls his r's, and discusses the Immortal Bard's "Ring of Rightness." Time seems to doze until one long noon when pipe smoke gathers about the professor like cumulous clouds rolling to a storm. Suddenly there is a puff and he is gone. Some say he went above and now sits near the Great White Throne impatient to be promoted out of his number two wings and into number three wings. Some say he went to a warmer place. Others say he never left and that his spirit haunts the university waiting to capture a bushy-tailed young instructor.

Whatever the truth may be, the L. Stafford Brown Reading Room is dedicated at the next commencement. The walls of the room are paneled in rich walnut, rescued from a mildewing English country house. Large stuffed red leather chairs cluster here and there. Along one wall stands an 18th century mahogany and rosewood bookcase. On its shelves are the professor's collection of cream pitchers. From above the mantlepiece, a mantlepiece on which, it is rumored, Dr. Johnson once rested a weary elbow while expostulating with Boswell, stares the professor himself. He appears walking across the Cotswolds. Sheep frisk behind him while in his right hand, he carries *the book*. In his left he holds a pipe. There are always a few bleary-eyed students in the room. Soon it is known as the Cave of the Old Sleeper.

The Books I Left Behind

Academics behave like hamsters. Instead, though, of stuffing their jowls with lettuce and raisins, and when the wind is in the east, their offspring, they lard houses with books—in the attic, in the basement, on top of the stereo in the living room, on a gold rack in the john. Occasionally, an academic will declare that he is going to stop cluttering his life with books. Don't believe him. Academics are worse off than a woe-begone sinner I heard testify in a tent meeting in Arkansas. Before settling down to heal the hopeless, the preacher called upon the congregation to witness to the power of the Spirit. A sister who looked like Hard Rock Mountain had fallen on her stood up. "Before I knew the Spirit," she said, "I used to get drunk every night and lie in the gutter with some strange man. Now," she continued, "I've almost quit."

Like the poor sister, the academic can almost quit books. For a while he might put bookstores behind him and testify that he is going to take a broom to his library. Not a volume, though, will ever appear in the garbage can. I am the only academic in the eastern United States to escape the bondage of books. It wasn't easy, but I did it. That preacher in Arkansas would be proud of me.

Not so long ago I moved from Dartmouth College to the University of Connecticut. Before leaving New Hampshire I shed more than six hundred volumes. Like a fat man who has jogged himself into a thin man, I feel better. My house is not a firetrap; squirrels don't build nests in the attic. Mice don't multiply in mildewed volumes in the basement, and all a visitor can find in the cabinet in the john is tooth paste, shaving cream, a pile of rusty razor blades, a bar of Zest, and four cans of "Pinewoods" Renuzit.

Books of literary criticism formed the biggest pile in the garbage can. Unless poisoned by university life, one outgrows literary criticism after thirty-five. Literary criticism is a matter of no importance. Wordsworth was right when he said that an impulse from a green wood could teach more about morality than all the sages. The person who reads books written by the Yale English department and is not made a fool by it is very lucky. Not even Billy Graham could save the Yale critics. In the future it will be easier for an elephant to crawl through a transom than it will for a book published by a university press to rest on my bookshelf. Innocents suckled on criticism in graduate school often lose all perspective. Like a tame barnyard cock, the young Ph.D. pecks about for years in the dirt until one day he publishes an article, flaps his wings, and makes a great commotion. His colleagues cackle and cluck as if he had turned up a pearl instead of a pale dunghill worm. Unless a fox runs away with his wife while he is scrabbling about in the dirt, the young teacher will ignore the world beyond the barnyard. Finding a comfortable roost in the chicken house, he will grow gray and waste his energies in profound but useless thinking. Never again shall scholarly truths crawl across a page before my eyes. Not even those I turned up myself. I threw away my dissertation, extra copies of my book, and a trunk overflowing with reprints of my articles.

As I grow old in an old century, I want warm books

snuggled about me like an eiderdown. I pitched crates of fiction. No longer will *Moby Dick* make me seasick or *Billy Budd* bring on a sore throat. Life is grim enough without *The Scarlet Letter*. Besides, gallantry of the sort which Hester Prynne enjoyed in her salad days is the favorite pastime of most people I know over thirty. William Dean Howells was right: good novels focus on the smiling aspects of life. Like vanilla ice cream and bluegrass marmalade, guilt and literature don't mix. The combination doesn't hurt the guilt, but it sure ruins the literature.

I also banished novelists whose first names are Thomas. Mann, Wolfe, and Hardy are all tainted by seriousness. So is Francis Bacon, and although I had misgivings I threw away *The Advancement of Learning*. A sensible man is dreadful company. He forever confines one to the hard asphalt of truth. Farrell, Dreiser, and Lewis are also fast fading from memory. Almost no contemporary fiction remains on my shelves. The small world of the neurotic is boring and self-indulgent. Meandering with Kim along the Grand Trunk Road from Benares to Lahore attracts me more than strumbling about through the back alleys of a broken psyche. The Valley of Melincourt from which Peacock's Sir Oran Haut-ton rescues weeping damsels is healthier than the suburban outpatient clinic. I prefer the Drones Club to Cottage Club and Bertie Wooster to Jake Barnes. Who cares about the beast which slumbers within when the Empress of Blandings lumbers without?

I kept novels which slope into the night like moon-lit sails. Happy endings are essential. I see enough bad endings in the daylight and don't want to confront them in the evening. Marriage always completes the good novel. Charles Dickens and Jane Austen make the heart leap up and bring

Christmas to the feelings. I have two editions of each. They glow in warm red leather where Russian novelists used to glower in yellow paper. Russian novelists, including Solzhenitsyn, have been exiled to a Siberia of the mind. Like all moralists Solzhenitsyn wants to save us from pleasure. The first volume of *The Gulag Archipelago* once ruined a stay at Sea Island, Georgia.

I began *The Gulag*, lounging in a folding chair under an umbrella on the beach. While I read, the sun moved across the sky, and before I knew it my legs broiled. That night my calves were swollen and bristly, resembling the trunks of coconut palms. Not even a regimen of Planter's Punch helped. My vacation was ruined. I could not go back on the beach. At night I had to wear Bermuda shorts; and no woman wants to dance with a man whose legs appear covered with prickly heat and who is wearing shorts, even if they are sporty Palm Beach shorts. If I had been reading Trollope, Fielding, Sterne, or Smollett, nights would have found me tripping the light fantastic toe. Throughout the reading delight would have seized me. I would have paused for smiles and laughter. Certain that God shined from his heaven, I would have looked up to drink in the beauty of the creation and would have noticed the sun on my legs.

Aside from Pnin and a maidenly Lolita, modern novels contain few characters I want to meet in the afterlife. My family is only second generation Episcopalian, and a lot of Christian still courses through my veins. Recently, I had a New England craftsman build me a pine coffin. Until I ripen for occupancy, however, I have had it fitted for book shelves. On them are novels which contain characters I would like to meet when I walk the golden streets. Sam Weller, Doctor Thorne, Toad of Toad Hall, Long John

Silver, Parson Adams, Lady Wishfort, Uncle Toby, Captain Cuttle, Pecksniff, Sophia Western, Emma Woodhouse, Humphry Clinker, Mr. Venus and his shop, and a host of other evergreen characters. Instead of being accompanied by my wife in suttee fashion—indeed once I am promoted to glory I would like to try out my wings and have a bit of a fling before settling down again to comfortable connubiality—I have instructed my heirs to paper the inside of my coffin with the title pages of my favorite books. As being slightly with child often leads to rounded pregnancy, so I hope the title pages will be the seeds of fullblown dreams.

Before I left New Hampshire, I gave away my Faulkners, Flannery O'Connors, Eudora Weltys, and Katherine Anne Porters. I don't disapprove of these writers. The grotesques which they describe are too familiar and resemble my high school friends. Just this past Christmas George Palmer's story was concluded. Poor George was afflicted with more intelligence than most students in my high school. In despair he tried to drink himself into normality. Unfortunately, he passed through cirrhosis of the liver and into the everlasting beyond with great alacrity. A retiring inhabitant of our vale of tears, George was known only for a green madras sport coat and was never seen without it. Near the end of his decline George married. Although he was only thirty-two, he embraced a mature spouse of fifty-six. She was a widow. Her late husband had owned a rental clothing store, and she carried on the business, hiring out paraphernalia for masquerades or morning suits for garden weddings. Mrs. Palmer did not, alas, enjoy George's company for long. Four months after their blessed matrimonial day, George rose to glory. This winter I needed a white tie for a ball. Of course I patronized the store run by the wife of a departed friend. While waiting to be fitted, I glanced through the costumes for rent. Gorillas, clowns, vampires, Arabs, werewolves, and Geishas hung in rows. One rack however, contained everyday clothes: suits and assorted jackets. As I looked at them, I noticed a green madras coat hanging near the end of the row. "It couldn't be," I thought. It was, and one could wear it for three dollars and 25 cents a day. "Mrs. Palmer," I said, when she came to fit me, "isn't that George's coat?" "Yes," she answered, "and every time I see it walking out the door I think of him, poor soul. Would you like to try it on? For one of George's friends I would lower the price. He would like it that way."

I didn't rent the jacket, but I got rid of novels containing southern grotesques. Perhaps I revolted against my background. Southerners grow up convinced that England is truth and truth is England. Suddenly I am tired of people whose heart is in the Cotswolds and think of Church Row in Hampstead every time they sing "Nearer My God to Thee." Southerners ought to come out of tour buses and declare themselves Americans. Leave England to Henry James and T. S. Eliot, whose books incidentally can no longer be found in my library.

From Eliot's *Collected Poems,* I razored out "The Hippopotamus." His description of the Hippopotamus slapping saints on the back and strumming a golden harp is almost worthy of Jerome K. Jerome. Religion has always interested me, and I kept the 1940 edition of the Episcopal hymnal. In one's late thirties, one goes to bed with many strange women, and the hymnal makes good bedtime reading. There are always a few hymns which strangers can sing together. After thirty-five, relationships with females change, so much so that the odd becomes mundane. Recently, as I started for the A & P to buy Diamond pecan halves and a jar of Hellmann's real mayonnaise for Waldorf salad, my telephone rang. It was Claire, a girl whom I had thought about marrying. She informed me that she was cracking up and could never see me again. "What," I said, thinking I had better hurry the conversation because the A & P would soon close. "Hmmm, very interesting," I continued as she described her symptoms. "I really must go," I finally said, urging her to take the sedative which her psychiatrist had prescribed, adding that I had an important appointment. I got to the A & P just before the doors were locked, bought the nuts and mayonnaise, and that evening whipped up a tasty salad.

Little poetry remains on my shelves. The truly civilized man carries himself with grace and dispenses wit with largesse at cocktail parties. All else, virtue, intelligence, is mere fume. I kept two anthologies of poetry so that I would be able to sparkle at the country club, greeting casual acquaintances with a negligent wave of the hand and an effervescent "Hail to thee blithe spirit" or responding to a hearty "Heard melodies are sweet" with a wink and a tripping "but those unheard are sweeter." Despite the insensitivity of anyone who could use a word so harsh as *palate*, much less describe bursting grapes thereupon, I almost kept a volume of Keats. Like all good reasons, mine was sentimental rather than intellectual. In heartier days I attended St. Catharine's College, Cambridge, and rowed five in assorted college boats. Martin Eason always rowed ahead of me at six. At boat club dinners, "Son" and I invariably tumbled into the sherry and the port. Occasionally Son almost drowned. When this occurred he would recite the entire "Ode to a Nightingale." The poem was his life raft; by the time he finished he was ready for more beakers tasting of flora and the night rapidly became less tender. Once while I lay beached with sherry lapping around my lips, Son tried to extinguish my right eye with a cigar. On another occasion he seized me, hung me around his shoulders, and we spun around like an airplane until we crashed over a television and through a door out into the clear night. Alas, youth does grow spectre-thin, and rowing boys pick themselves up from the grass. Son is now a minister in the north of England, wrestling with the devil instead of me.

Although rational people outgrow sentimental, familial ties, I kept the third and fourth books of *Childe Harold*. When I was small, my father used to read me Byron's description of the Colosseum and the dying gladiator. For a similar reason, though, I threw away the Horatio Hornblower novels which father gave me. They were an emblem of the discrepancy between life led and life dreamed. In 1929 when he was twenty years old, my father graduated from college. Immediately he went to work for the Travelers Insurance Company. After that, he never traveled. At night he read adventure novels and dreamed of faraway lands where flying fishes played. He never saw a faraway land or a flying fish. Instead he received two watches from the Travelers, one after he had worked for twenty-five years and another when he retired after forty-three years. Engraved on the back of the last one was the Travelers Tower in Hartford, as if Hartford and that gray building, not sweeter, greener lands, were objects of all aspiration.

When I attended college, I was like most undergraduates, too young and innocent to learn much. Characters rather than ideas impressed me. The man who taught Romantic poetry drove an old Buick; in its trunk he kept a spade and a complete Wordsworth. Whenever he saw a colorful wild-flower, he would stop, dig it up, carry it home, and replant it in his garden. For him, the meanest flower that blew conveyed thoughts. In his classes the sad music of humanity rang out clearly, unencumbered by brittle intellectuality. On my desk now sits a complete Wordsworth. To it I have owed sensations sweet, felt in the blood and passing into the heart with tranquil restoration.

Compared to biography, poetry occupies a large part of my library. Human beings are too complex to be laid out on a page like a patient etherized upon a table. No biographer can finally know his subject, and no biography can be definitive. Only the ignorant, the naïve, and the young believe that another person is ultimately knowable. In graduate school I bought and read many biographies, including the first three volumes of Leon Edel's *Henry James*. I never purchased Edel's two other volumes. Before the Flood, as Sydney Smith put it, when man lived seven hundred years, he could spend a decade reading a book. The Flood contracted man's life span to three score and ten years. Mr. Edel should have looked at the ark and been wise. In any case the three volumes of the James biography and all the other biographies which I owned have now been recycled.

Unfortunately, the sins of the first printing are probably visited upon the second and they have become dictionaries. Before I left New Hampshire I threw away my two volume *Oxford English Dictionary* when the magnifying glass broke. It was a fortunate break. I have put much thought and work into simplifying my life. Complexity results from a failure of will. With its interminable lists of meanings, the OED confuses and imposes complexity upon definition.

General use of the OED by all classes would lead to every species of folly. There would not be a madhouse in the country in which a considerable number of the inhabitants had not been driven there by the book's extravagance. Government would be impossible and the nation would become a vast asylum for incurables. Along with the OED I also pitched my French, Latin, and German dictionaries. In academic circles foreign languages are useless, except for the occasional and well-enunciated "Je ne sais quoi."

Age brings understanding of the useful and the useless. Teachers tell children that the study of particular subjects will enable them to live better lives as adults. The advice is always wrong. Unfortunately, one learns this only after spending long hours beneath the lamp. "A knowledge of history," the child is informed, "enables the individual and indeed the state to learn from and thereby avoid the mistakes of the past." No individual, much less nation, profits from the past. Thankfully, man is blessed to go on his way doing as he has always done. Moreover, it is almost impossible to determine just what man has done in the past. Not even literary criticism is more subjective than history. The father of lies was the first historian, and through apostolic succession his mantle has passed into the present. Still history has an anecdotal value. Although I threw away Thucydides, Gibbon, Macaulay, Namier, and a complete set of the Oxford History of England, I kept Herodotus, Plutarch, Suetonius, and Carlyle. Carlyle's is the only account of the French Revolution not marred by pretension to truth.

If what the world calls useful is not useless, it is vulgar. I threw away all the "how to" books and etiquette manuals which presumptuous friends and a solicitous family had given me. I will never be my own repair man. The inner gurglings of televisions, refrigerators, and septic tanks mystify me. Insofar as I know an angel lurks under the hood of my car, not what the cognoscenti call an internal combustion engine. Furthermore, I have no desire to study body mechanics. On an informal night school basis I have learned enough about such matters to last several lifetimes. With relief, I threw away those books which clinically describe the extraordinary activities of Himalayan tribesmen. After thirty-five, unless one enjoys visiting the chiropractor, one should concentrate on detumescent prose. Aside from a few rules to hold barbarity at a distance, the matter in etiquette manuals is unimportant. Yeats was wrong. More often than not custom and ceremony destroy rather than nurture innocence and beauty. Etiquette books do not teach people to become insiders; they teach how to make others outsiders. They exclude rather than include and destroy spontaneity and creativity. When whiskey is not going to be served at a wedding reception, I avoid the wedding. Never, however, do I write, "Samuel Pickering, Jr. regrets that he will be unable to attend the marriage of . . ." Instead I use the occasion to write a personal letter rich with embellishments. Recently I was unable to attend a ceremony in Atlanta because a friend who had just escaped from rebels in Chad was visiting me. He was now in the process, I informed the hostess of trying to extricate the four swarthy children he had been forced to sire while a prisoner.

Books, if they are inscribed presents, are particularly difficult to get rid of. But I did—some thirty volumes across the title pages of which ran inscriptions whose style ranged from circular female intimacy to angular academic spite. Jettisoning gift books is particularly satisfying. For a moment one believes he is escaping the hackneyed commonplace of personal identity. I took great pleasure in dropping into the garbage can Kahlil Gibran's *The Prophet,* the first gift book I received in high school. When I was sixteen, a brunette cheerleader with whom I was on hand-holding terms presented it to me during the football season and lovingly inscribed it, "To my dearest Cuddles." That girl will never know the agony she caused. One of my teammates saw the inscription. For the entire fall, my classmates, the members of the team, even the coach called me Cuddles. When *The Prophet* fell into the can, I felt like Christian at the Cross, free from a lifetime of burdens.

Akin to gift books were those books which I autographed myself. In the past I never bought a book without inscribing it. I delighted in stunning undergraduates with the wide range of my acquaintances and in bringing out my books at dinner parties when all the guests had reached rosy befuddlement. Hemingway and I watched baseball together, and "Big Ernie" wrote in my copy of *In Our Time,* "Always throw hardballs Sam." Bill Faulkner wrote, "Laddiebuck, if only Caddy had met you when she was fifteen." Wallace Stevens wrote graciously, "My everlasting thanks to the man who corrected so many of my poems in manuscript." Poignantly, Percy Shelley wrote, "To Sam who has spent many hours trying to teach me to swim—affectionately, Shells." When I showed this last inscription to the brightest graduate student I knew at Princeton, she exclaimed, "My God, Sam, you knew Shelley! Why haven't you said anything before now?" "Modesty," I answered and beat a hasty retreat. Nowadays such incidents don't rise to the funny bone so quickly as they used to. I've known Shells, Big Ernie, Bill, Wallace, and a hundred more all too well. With relief, almost as if I were escaping family, I stacked the autographed books outside for the trash man.

I cleared my bookshelves with the passion of a sand-hill parson fondling a comely sinner. Gone are all my college textbooks and their embarrassing marginalia. So are the *Iliad*, the *Odyssey*, and Shakespeare. Blackguards of the first water, worse than the Khmer Rouge, inhabit the first two books. As for Shakespeare, his plays must be seen to be understood. Besides, no academic reads Shakespeare regularly; it just isn't done. Even those who teach him rarely read the plays, preferring instead to graze across criticism. While raging through my library like Attila in Central Asia, I did spare some volumes. Although places and occasionally people matter to me, I have never taken a photograph in my life. Instead I buy coffee table books containing pictures of my favorite places: Prague, Leningrad, Petra, Jerusalem, Rhodes, Budapest. Leningrad with its bone-white columns yellowing in the pale sun streams into countless associations: eighteen days in a row at the Kirov and then Dzerzhinsky's *Fate of a Man*. Performed for a Sunday matinee, the only time in the week Russians were not pushed aside for tourists and Western currency, *Fate of a Man* is a Soviet opera, describing the life of a common soldier during the Second World War. By the end of the opera, the man had lost home and family. While flames flickered in the background, he stood distraught among the ruins, not only of his life but of Russia herself. Then among the rubble he found a starving child. Reaching down he picked up the boy. Cradling him in his arms and singing all the while, the soldier crossed a bridge which had been suspended above the orchestra pit. Down the aisle of the Kirov he strode singing.

When he went out the back and the opera ended, no one applauded. But then I looked around. This was Leningrad. The house was full of old men and women who could not forget the war. Tears ran in torrents. Even I almost wept— not for the Russians, they mattered little to me—but for myself. I knew that nothing: no work of art, no love, no horror could ever make me weep in public.

I also kept the memoirs of and books by several posturers and liars like Trelawny and Richard Halliburton. Academics feel close to such people. To be a successful teacher, preacher, or country music singer, one has to have a bit of Trelawny in him. I kept several essayists: Lamb, Hazlitt, and Sydney Smith, with his sound advice to take cold baths and hope for the best. I even have Cobbett's *Rural Rides* although I know I'll never read it again. I also have *The Anatomy of Melancholy;* I have never read it, but it is a wonderful commonplace book. I kept Gilbert and Sullivan, although other humorists like Freud, Marx, and the Lawrences, D. H. and T. E., made the little list of writers whom I'll never miss. With regret, I banished Twain. His cynicism has a dangerous way of burrowing through the skin, dropping into the bloodstream, and becoming incurable. Still whenever I read the newspaper I think of Pudd'nhead Wilson when he said he wished he owned half of an objectionable dog. When asked what he would do with his half, he said he would kill it. Today most of the dogs are gathered in Washington. You'd have to go some, though, to buy even a smidgen of one. The AMA, NRA, AFL-CIO, Boeing, Lockheed, General Motors, Mobil, Exxon, etc. have cornered the canine market.

I also have a family Bible. It is difficult to throw away a Bible. Although I did get rid of nine others, I kept the

oldest and biggest. It was filled with locks of hair, wedding
and funeral invitations, and Confederate money. Early this
fall I put in a black-eyed Susan which Claire gave me. In
ten years, will I remember it? I'm not sure how much of
the Bible I'll read in the future. The heroes of the Old
Testament seem to be the first cousins of the scoundrels
who besieged Troy. Sometimes I have nightmares about
climbing Jacob's Ladder and being met at the top by
David, eager for me to collaborate with him on the definitive, annotated edition of the Psalms.

The only part of my library that remained relatively un-
disturbed was that devoted to children's books. Like Wordsworth's poetry, fairy tales seem forever fresh. By describing
a world of transformations fairy tales beguile away the long
night and charm the shadows that darken the day. I kept
many children's books: *The Wind in the Willows* for Ratty's
"messing about in boats"; *Horton Hatches the Egg* for its
wonderful depiction of the dreamer sitting day after day
and then hatching the impossible; *Ferdinand the Bull* for
the cork tree and flowers far from the fret of life; and
Uncle Remus for Brer Rabbit, the little man who triumphs
over the foxes of the world. With regret, I threw away *The
Little Engine that Could*. For a child sure of immortality
and whose heart leaps up when he beholds a rainbow in the
sky, it is a joyful book. For a man beyond thirty-five, a
marriage or two, and an eternity of hopes, the Little Engine
steams along on heartache.

Well, that's the story of the books I left behind. I know
I will regret leaving some. Tonight, though, I'm stretching
out with *Uncle Fred in the Springtime*. It's hot stuff, just
the sort of thing to make one forget winter and a cold,
lonely house. Mustard Pott, Pongo Twistleton, Horace

Davenport, and Sir Roderick Glossop are down at Blandings Castle livening up the old rock pile. Later I'll read Charles Lamb, not "Dream Children," however. The last time I read it, I called Claire. The line was busy. Fate often hangs on the telephone company's fragile wires. After the call, I threw away the address book with her phone number in it. I think I can forget the number if I give up Waldorf salad.

Old Things and New Baby

I cannot remember when I did not want old things. Mother says that her youth offended me when I was a child. She thinks my grandmother should have been my mother. Maybe she is right. I recall envying a friend who went to live with his grandmother in a wonderful old house after his parents died. The entrance hall resembled a tunnel and stern ancestors looked down from the walls. An early American sideboard loured on one side while eight square-backed Hepplewhite chairs stood rigid along the other. Shadows hung everywhere and my friend avoided the hall. It was my favorite place in the house. On rainy days when we played hide-and-go-seek inside, I always hid under the sideboard.

I still play hide-and-go-seek. Whenever I visit someone's home for the first time, I soon slip away. While other guests gather over drinks or conversation, I search for things more intoxicating. Usually I find them in the china cabinet. There I gaze at Rose Medallion or Staffordshire. Bearded cats tease me like a mouse out of thought while hesitant, deferential mandarins in green coats and red trousers make me dream of warm days at the summer palace.

Collectors are different from other people. I have known this a long time. As a boy I spent summers on my grandfather's dairy farm in Hanover, Virginia. Near my grandfather lived a recluse named Mason Jefferson. There was nothing remarkable about Old Man Jefferson, as he was called, until two lightning rods appeared on the roof of his house one summer. The next summer there were six; then there were nine. Soon after I arrived from Tennessee, Henry and James Hackenbridge, sons of my grandfather's herdsman and my constant companions, would take me on an expedition to Mr. Jefferson's house. We would stand barefoot in the dirt road and count lightning rods. One summer when the number had grown to fourteen and counting was difficult, we climbed Mr. Jefferson's fence to get a better view. Mr. Jefferson saw us, came out on the porch, and asked what we were doing. James answered that we were looking at the lightning rods and then unaccountably bold, he asked Mr. Jefferson why he had so many. Mr. Jefferson said, "I like lightning rods" and went back inside. James said he thought the old man was crazy, but I recognized a kindred spirit. Mr. Jefferson was a collector, and although I would not have wanted new lightning rods on my roof, I understood why Mr. Jefferson bought them.

The summers I spent in Virginia helped make me a collector. At a time when there are no undiscovered lands, collectors may be the last adventurers. Instead of dark continents we explore dark attics. Instead of catching yaws or schistosomiasis, we stump our toes and bark our shins against the past's agreeable clutter. In grandfather's attic, clothes draped from the rafters like Spanish Moss and trunks were strewn across the floor like broken columns. Forgotten treasure lay hidden behind every corner or buried at the bottom of each trunk. I did not need Long John Silver and the *Hispaniola* to take me to far-off lands for pieces of eight. Nearer home I discovered fabulous pieces of plate. Once these had been in the White House of the Confederacy in Richmond. Mended they now sit on a chest in my living room—except on April 9, the day Lee surrendered at Ap-

pomatox Courthouse. That night I eat an old-fashioned
meal off them, country ham, batter bread, stewed tomatoes,
greens, if I can get them, and watermelon rind pickle, the
kind of meal that most of Lee's soldiers must have dreamed
of returning home to but which few enjoyed.

Collectors of old things are invariably old-fashioned.
Hand-me-downs from my father and grandfathers, my neck-
ties never expand or shrink with the season. Like Penelope
waiting for Ulysses to return from Troy, my lapels remain
constant while the cuffs of my trousers catch enough lint
for her to complete two tapestries. My shirts are white and
no alligators, bears, or rabbits crawl or hop across my
bosom. I do not own a television. Collectors collect not
simply things but people and stories. Without a story attached a possession is incomplete. The drama of searching
and buying fills a collector's days and nights, leaving no
time for television. Collecting does not separate a person
from life; it thrusts him into it. Instead of basking like a
lizard fat and greasy in the sun during his vacation, the
collector explores a jungle of shops, seeking to "bring it
back" to liven up his life. Wooden-spooled screens from
Aswan isolate my breakfast table from the kitchen. Behind
the screens I forget stainless efficiency and imagine Luxor
and Karnack and paddlewheelers treading the Nile. A vi-
tamin pill goes down unnoticed as feluccas sweep like swal-
lows along the table.

With colors and patterns jostling against each other, the
rugs on my floors recall the Hamadeus souk in Damascus
where I found them. One glance and they fill the dreariest
winter evening with the sounds of buying and selling:
vendors carrying brass cans of honeyed rose water on their
backs, bedouin women in black and red with trays of sweets

on their heads, scabrous small boys with armfuls of plastic bags or cap pistols, carts brimming with cashews, pecans, oranges, fool, eggplant, okra—life itself clamoring to be seen and heard. In my study is an ivory and mother of pearl dowry chest from Aleppo. Four feet tall and five feet long and weighing more than two hundred and fifty pounds, its garish solidity contrasts with the delicate fragility of the sacrament it celebrates. Possessions, not preachers, teach collectors that appearances deceive. A samovar squats on the dowry chest, its front patterned by the double eagle of the Romanoffs and the names of cities in whose expositions it won prizes: Brussels, Paris, and Milan. The samovar rests on an iron base and seems secure; yet like Imperial Russia, it is hollow and top-heavy and a slight push could tumble it to the floor.

In collecting the race is to the swift and the decisive. If collectors governed the world, it would be a healthier place. Aware that delay leads to loss, collectors would not let situations drift aimlessly from bad to worse to blood. When my great Aunt Lula died in a rotting Victorian house on the wrong side of Nashville, I cancelled my classes at the University of Connecticut and flew to Nashville in hopes of beating the burglars to her attic. There I found the sheet music to a group of songs published by the "Nashville Patriot Press." Along the staircase in my house now hang the scores of "The Forrest Shottish Dedicated To The General And His Staff," the "Cavalry Galop, Dedicated To Texas Rangers," the "Lexington Quickstep Dedicated To Gen. Price," and the "Shiloh Victory Polka Dedicated To The Heroes Of The Battle Of Pittsburg Landing." Above my desk are receipts given to my cousin Enoch Brown in Franklin, Tennessee by General Hood's quartermaster when the Army of Tennessee passed through Williamson County on the way to its grave at Nashville.

Utilitarians and social reformers frequently accuse collectors of being selfish and indulgent. We are told that we neglect man's responsibility for man and contribute little to the public good. The truth is far different. The receipts which I found in Aunt Lula's attic settled an argument which threatened to disrupt a dinner party. When two acquaintances began to argue over whether or not tobacco was grown in Middle Tennessee before 1880, I excused myself, went upstairs, and returned with one of the receipts. On December 15, 1864, the Army of Tennessee bought 2166 pounds of tobacco from Enoch Brown. At seventy-five cents a pound, the tobacco was worth $1624.50; alas, it was "not paid for."

Collectors soon learn that ours is a little world made cunningly. With not only his tobacco, but also ten young hogs estimated to weigh 1700 pounds appropriated and not paid for, Christmas 1864 was not a happy time for Cousin Enoch. Although a Confederate victory at Nashville would have brought Enoch his money, it would have been disastrous for the Union and probably for me. My great-grandfather William Blackstone Pickering fought in the Battle of Nashville on the other side. A farm boy from near Athens, Ohio, he enlisted as a cavalryman and eventually became General Thomas's secretary at Nashville. In my study are his Colt pistol, his war diary, and the pen with which one Colonel Mitchener signed his commission. Collecting makes a person tolerant. North and South, Yankee and Rebel mix peacefully on the walls of my house. No collector needs affirmative action to teach him the wonders and benefits of diversity. From cultural mixtures come life, beauty, and understanding. In my dining room a Herend owl perches near David Roberts's Petra in a manner that is graceful and fitting, although ornithologically impossible. If the lamb no longer lies down with the lion in our fallen world, at least my Rockingham dog never chases my Staffordshire cats. Ethnic, social, and theological differences do not erect barriers between people in the world of the figurine. On the shelves of my secretary no man is more or less than the clay out of which he was created. In a dark frock coat and with his right hand on a pile of sealed deeds, William Penn stands dignified yet comfortable and content alongside black-faced Thomas Dartmouth Rice, jumping Jim Crow at the Surrey Theatre. A primitive Welch Baptist, the Reverend Christian Evans had only one eye. Like his vision his theology was narrow; yet in my secretary he does not look askance at the right hand extended to him by "The Apostle of Temperance," Father Theobald Mathew, a gentle Irish priest who persuaded huge numbers of Irishmen to renounce spirits in the 1830s and 40s.

Dinner in the home of a non-collector is more arid than the Gobi. Conversation always drifts to the fashionably routine: the latest novel, ecology, or the sexual doings of youth or of other athletic but ill-informed primitives. At such a home even the lemon soufflé suffers from *petite mal* and collapses in a soggy heap. Far different is an evening with a collector. Anecdotes spice both conversation and food. Interested in his collections, the host has no time for mundane causes or celebrities. Like the bubbles which rise from champagne and hint at a quick flavor, the anecdotes of a collector tickle guests' palates and create a satisfyingly warm atmosphere. Not long ago a collector specializing in uniquely-bound, autographed first editions invited me to dinner at his home in Warren, New Hampshire. While he prepared the meal, the other guests and I browsed through his remarkable library. At dinner when I asked him where he discovered his Dickens collection, including an inscribed copy of Kate Dickens's cookbook, he merely waved his right hand carelessly, passed me the Chinese vegetables, and said, "oh, those old things." We were startled. Like a carp after doughballs, a collector rarely fails to rise open-mouthed to an anecdote. Collectors' lives, though, resemble attics. The more one explores, the more one finds. At dinner the surprise did not lie locked away at the bottom of an eighteenth century campaign chest but hung under the table. During the meal when someone made a clever re-mark, our host leaned forward as if he were laughing. Sud-denly bells began to ring. Besides books, it seemed, our host collected old bells. Beneath the center of the table were seventy-seven. A series of wires attached them to levers at the head of the table. The cleverer the remark, the more intricate the bell ringing. This was not all however. As the forum in Rome and pyramids at Giza, so our host had not simply sound but sound and light. On low tables around the walls of the dining room lay a glittering selection of the host's glass paperweight collection. Under each paper-weight, though we did not know it, was a hole; in the hole was a small lightbulb. When someone made a particularly good remark, our host threw a switch and lights began to flash under the paperweights. Like brandy the effect was magical, and our conversation outshot the frailty of the moment, ranging over the hills and far away.

Collectors are too busy for ordinary activities like court-ing or watching football. Like many of my friends, I as-sumed I would end, to use an old phrase, "on the shelf" next to my possessions. Four years ago, however, while shopping for samplers in a little store outside Princeton, I met another collector. When she discovered that I shared her interest, she invited me to see her collection of Adam and Eve, Tree of Knowledge samplers. She had put some of the best between layers of glass and then had them made into the tops of tables. I asked her to introduce me to the craftsman who made the tables and I ordered one. Building the table took time. Not only did I have to fetch a sampler from Connecticut but I also wanted him to refinish a worm-eaten mahogany kneehole library table that I had rescued from my grandmother's basement. Restoration was difficult and I had to make several trips to New Jersey.

For the experienced collector owning an item is often not so pleasurable as thinking about possessing it. Occasionally a knowing collector can indulge in the sybaritic luxury of a week's debate. "I will put this away for you, sir" are the sweetest sounds a collector can hear. For once the pleasures of poverty outweigh the rewards of wealth. Counting nickels and dimes, starting to the shop then turning back, the collector lives a life of sensations. The longer he is able to put off buying, the more enjoyable the purchase is. Unfortunately my friend made me forget technique and like a green, unseasoned collector I rushed in, ready to pay any price for her and her samplers. After a year and a half, I won my friend and her collection. Although she was not old like everything else in my house, she was not new, being almost twenty-seven, and I planned that we would spend happy years together increasing our collections.

For over a year we did just that. I arranged to teach in Syria and we spent weekends and long vacations exploring shops in the Mideast. The life of a long-distance collector like that of a marathon runner is exhausting, and when we returned home, it seemed natural for my wife to sleep a great deal in order to catch up. Busy with a new interest in Chinese snuff bottles, I paid little attention until she fell asleep while we were going to an exhibition of Balch school samplers in Worcester, Massachusetts. Since tsetse flies are rarely seen in Connecticut, I was convinced she must have picked up encephalitis or some other exotic ailment during our last days in Aswan. The next Monday I took her to a doctor. After examining her, he brought me into his office and said, "Mr. Pickering, I have some good news. You can soon expect a little bundle of joy." "What," I thought, "was that dealer in Farmington prepared to accept my reasonable, albeit somewhat less than inflationary, offer for his snuff bottles?" Yellow and green, blue and red, each seemed a small Eden, full of budding flowers. Woe is me—although the bundle to which the doctor referred was small it was not old. Instead of coming wrapped in soft colors, it appears, I understand, in bright pink and is not at all comfortable in a corner cupboard.

Miss Lucy Cidner lived across the street from my paternal grandfather in Carthage, Tennessee. One day after picking a bucket of strawberries, my grandfather saw Miss Lucy sitting on her front porch, rocking and fanning herself. Knowing she liked strawberries, grandfather poured out a pint and walked across the street to give them to her. When he reached the front steps, Miss Lucy put down her fan, stopped rocking, and said, "Mr. Sam, I am glad you came by. I have just had a nervous breakdown." "I am sorry," said grandfather, "but I have brought you some strawberries." "That's nice of you, Mr. Sam, thank you," Miss

Lucy said as she took the strawberries. After grandfather left, Miss Lucy washed the strawberries and poured cream over them and sat on the front porch and ate them. When she finished, she began to rock and fan herself again. Like Miss Lucy the collector soon learns to control his emotions. The eager bird never gets the bargain worm. As a result collectors are usually patterns of soft Wedgewood gentility. Like Adamesque chairs their emotions flow in gentle curves and the unexpected rarely causes angularity. After talking to the doctor, I smiled, went home and began rocking on the front porch. I knew that china and children did not mix. The next day I removed the old things from the living room, and, after boxing them carefully, carried them to the attic. The room looked more barren than Iran. For a month I rocked on the front porch. Unlike china one could not hold a child up to the light to look for tell-tale brown lines. If one did, there was likely to be, as a rude friend informed me, "an unfortunate accident."

In an age which celebrates change, collectors are repositories of true sanity. As they treasure and do not let old things disappear, so old habits do not die easily in them. One day as I drove near Farmington, I found myself approaching the shop where I discovered the snuff bottles. Cluttered with neglected pieces of the past, such shops play with the imagination and awaken memories. A yellowing antimacassar reminds the collector of his grandmother's parlor with its carved walnut spoon-back settee and Gone With the Wind lamps. For the collector the part evokes a whole. A rusted box of "Dr. Johnson's Educator Crackers" becomes a vision of a country store with the post office in one corner and a tiger cat sleeping in another.

Knowing the snuff bottles would be gone, I felt melancholy when I entered the shop. Along with the dust, my spirits soon lifted, however, as I began rummaging through boxes in the back storeroom. A collector cannot rock on the porch for long; too many things will attract his attention. In the shop I found something wonderful, a toy cannon made in Germany before the First World War. Later in a shop in Manchester I found a toy Model-T army truck. These two and a convoy of others now sit where I once kept the Rose Medallion china. I hope the baby will like them; if not, maybe he will like my father's little red wagon. He gave it to me when I was small and it followed me everywhere overflowing with kittens, puppies, rocks, and mock oranges. My wife does not sleep much any more. She says the baby will be a girl and is busy restoring a dollhouse which her grandfather made. She wants me to learn to sew so that I can repair her dolls. Since we don't know if the baby will be a boy or a girl, I am not going to learn. Maybe we will have twins; then both of us can continue building our collections of toys. Perhaps we will even begin a collection of children. Since children are not "old things," I have dusted off some forgotten family names. That should start them out old and right.

Reading at Forty

March in my part of Connecticut is bleak. There is much cold rain and wind, and the ground is grey and muddy. Flowers don't appear until April, and earthworms are the only sign of spring. After a rainy night, they lie full and soft on sidewalks. By afternoon, the wind has dried them, and they are brittle and dark and look like small sticks. The sight bothers me, and on wet mornings, I leave for work a little early. Whenever I see an earthworm on the sidewalk, I pick it up and carry it to higher, drier ground. People have seen me doing this, and some have come to my office to ask the reason. I have a ready answer. "All my life I have suffered from earaches," I say, taking a notecard from my desk and reading it, "at least until I discovered this remedy in Thomas Lupton's *A Thousand Notable things of sundrie sortes* (1627): 'Earth wormes fried with Goose greace, then straind, and a little thereof dropt warme into the deafe or pained eare,'" I read, "'doth help the same.'" "Oh," people usually say, and then we laugh and talk about medicine or the weather. Of course I don't know why I save worms; it just seems the right thing to do. Ten years ago I would not have done it. I would have walked briskly to work, and instead of noticing the worms, would have crushed them under foot as I thought about the day ahead. Over the past few years though, I have slowed and becoming less intense now see things I never saw before.

Since childhood, I have been a reading man, rushing

through print. More than anything else, perhaps, my reading has changed as I have grown older, and like the earthworms plucked from the sidewalk and carried to safer
ground, I have drifted to the soft shoulder of time. I read
slowly now, and instead of burning through pages searching for truth, I vagabond along the margin, hoping I will
stumble across a neglected book which will momentarily
transform the ordinary into something magical. Once I
read with purpose and in pursuit of light followed arduous
schedules. Belief in systematic approaches to life, much less
systematic reading, however, disappears with age. Indeed,
as one grows older and discovers that words create rather
than mirror or explain reality, all quests for truth seem beside the point. Unlike young people who read for content
and who neglect form, the older reader celebrates appearance, for he suspects that appearance may be the only absolute. University courses in great books suit the young
student whose experience is limited and who believes that
reading will not only give him direction but will also
determine success. After forty, one rarely discusses great
books; coping with daily living does not leave much energy
for being concerned with, for example, the motives and
sufferings of an Anna Karenina. "All that strumpet needed,"
a friend declared recently, "was a good spanking. Look,"
he said, "she doesn't interest me. I've got to sow grass seed
today and the yard is covered with sticks. When you spend
your time picking up sticks and worrying about scraping
the car every time you back out of the garage, Anna
Karenina's doings don't mean very much." Once when I
lived in a bookish land in which tragedy was an everyday
affair and ogres swollen with passion and appetite stalked
the streets, my friend's statement would have bothered me.

Now I simply thought about the weeds in my own front yard and the dent I put in my car at the A & P. As earthworms now seemed important to me, so my friend's concentration upon little, familiar things appeared both decorous and sensible.

Although I do not believe that reading can determine behavior, I, nevertheless, avoid books which celebrate intemperance. As I now sprinkle two teaspoons of Brewer's Yeast over my cereal in the morning in hopes of smoothing out my diet, so I enjoy books which describe healthy lives. Occasionally, though, I stray from health foods and healthy books. Sometime ago, my wife Vicki and I spent a year in Syria. The only books in English we could find in our town were paperback editions of D. H. Lawrence. Reading Lawrence was disquieting. Below the front of our apartment, the Mediterranean stretched peacefully out to the horizon in blue ribbons, while from the back, snow-covered mountains of southern Turkey seemed to hang down from the sky in a grey haze. Our days were cool and green, and like those of most congenial married couples, our hours were satisfyingly filled with ordinary living: wandering through the cluttered streets or shopping in the open markets. Lawrence's men and women behaved differently. Instead of the soft shades that colored our lives, their world seemed garishly bright. "These people," I said to Vicki as I put down *Lady Chatterley's Lover*, "suffer from spring fever throughout the year." "Not spring fever," she answered; "they have caught swine flu and there's no vaccination." "No vaccination, perhaps," I said, "but there are cures."

As a person ages, he reads more for play than for meaning. Often when I meet feverish characters, like those in Lawrence's books, I set about finding cures for their problems. Vicki and I stopped in London on our way home from Syria so that I could accomplish some research. If Chatterley had been a reading man like me, and paid attention to his diet as I do to mine, his wife would not have taken her love to the woodlands. "Partriche," Thomas Elyot wrote in *The Castell of Helth* (1541), "reviveth luste, which is abated" while the brains of "sparowes" although they "be harde to digeste . . . stireth up Venus." If Chatterley like many British were sentimental about and refused to eat birds, he could have added green grapes to his meals, for they, Thomas Paynell wrote in 1597, "augment rising of a man's yard." Of course the cause of Chatterley's marital deficiency might not have been physical but psychological, or to use a synonym "supernatural." For this, Thomas Lupton happily provided a remedy. "If a married man," he wrote, "be let or hindered through Inchantment, Sorcerie or Witchcraft, from the acte of generation, let him make water through his marriage Ring, and he shall be loosed from the same, and their doings shall have no further power in him." On the other hand, Chatterley might have found the tepid relationship with his wife comfortable and only been disturbed by Mellors's untoward activities. To have changed Mellors's behavior would have been relatively simple for a reading man. "Hemlocks bound to a mans stones," Humphrie Lloyd wrote in *The Treasury of Health* (1585), "take utterly away all desire of copulation." In the event, quite likely because he was comparatively uneducated, that Mellors refused to follow the example of Socrates and take his medicine, Chatterley could have discovered a more subtle approach in William Turner's *Herbal* (1568). Having first instructed Mellors to plant artichokes in the garden, he could then have graciously given them to him when they were ripe. Indeed, it was extremely important for Mellors to enjoy them all and to keep them from Lady Chatterley, for, Turner observes, as the artichoke "provoketh lust in women so it abateth the same in men."

The reading I do for research is not limited to the problems of fictional characters but also focuses on those of actual individuals. If Oscar Wilde had read proper books when he was young, he might have talked less and lived a better life. For some time I have searched for the right book to send Wilde's parents. This past summer, I found it, *First Impressions; or, The History of Emma Nesbit* (1814). Like Oscar, Emma talked too much and betrayed confidences. After her carelessness hurt a friend, she determined to reform and did well until the morning of a fancy dress ball. Emma's father was a banker and being temporarily short of money could not buy her a dress. Rather than wear an old outfit, Emma decided to miss the ball and stay at school. Then an acquaintance, Jane Turner, came to Emma's room and asked what she was wearing to the ball. When Emma said she was not going, Jane exclaimed, "are you mad? why what in the world is to prevent your going?" On learning that Emma's father would not buy her a new dress, Jane said he must be "shamefully stingy." Rather than hear her father wrongfully accused of being penurious, Emma betrayed a family confidence and explained the reason he could not buy a dress. Jane immediately left the room and sent a message to her aunt, urging her to withdraw her money from Mr. Nesbit's bank. "Draw directly on Mr. Nesbit for all the money he has of yours," she wrote, "and then, if the house stop payment the next hour, it will be of no consequence to you." Jane's aunt followed her niece's instructions; a run started on the bank and by late afternoon, it had failed. Emma's mother who had told her about her father's difficulties then "fell into a state of despondency, from which nothing could rouse her, and expired soon after in the arms of her husband."

As one ages and learns to use words well, proving almost any assertion about literature or life becomes easy. As a result research ceases to be a serious matter and becomes a game. Neglected books and odd statements come to furnish life better than artificial intellectuality. Once my study was clean and well-lit; now it is shadowy, and bits of things clutter it: a picture of my great-grandfather at twenty as a Union soldier, an eighteenth-century leather mastiff collar, a hundred year old flower garden quilt, a fruitwood scoop with a handle shaped like the tail feathers of a chicken, and a rusty grease pan used to catch drippings from a spit. I found these things by rummaging through shops and attics. Similarly by reading through libraries I have discovered and collected an odd group of quotations. I keep them on cards in boxes that appear to be a set of Bulwer bound in green leather. Instead of facts with which to buttress an interpretation, research now brings me statements which glow warm and eccentrically personal. Whenever I decide that spring will never come to Connecticut, I read my excerpts from *The First Dixie Reader* (1863) by Mrs. C. B. Moore and know why I left Tennessee. "Uncle Ned," Mrs. Moore wrote, "was a good old dar-key and lov-ed his mas-ter well. They liv-ed near the Yank-kee lines, and when the Yan-kee ar-my come, old Ned and his wife and children, went a-way with them. They told Ned that he should be free, and live like white folks; but he soon found they had not told him the truth. He did not fare so well as he did at home with his mas-ter."

This past year "Life on Earth" was on television. I started to watch it, but soon found it dull and stopped. None of the creatures described were as marvellous as those that lurk on the cards behind *A Strange Story*. According to Samuel Goodrich's *Anecdotes of the Animal Kingdom* (1845), a gentleman in Salisbury, England, kept a pet oyster which he fed oatmeal. The oyster, Goodrich wrote, "proved itself an excellent mouser, having killed five mice, by crushing the heads of such as, tempted by the meal, had the audacity to intrude their noses within its bivalvular clutches." My latest acquisition comes from *The History of Mr. Rightway and his Pupils* (1816). At the Siege of Burgos, Mr. Rightway's brother, Major Rightway, "fell victim to the ruthless and indiscriminate scythe of war." In the same battle the major's servant was killed and the servant's son Dennis, a drummer boy, lost a leg. In describing Burgos to Mr. Rightway, Dennis stated, "I lost my father, and his good honour the Major at the blackguard place, which carried away my leg at the same time; but I afterwards saw it buried in the same grave with my father, and that's some comfort."

Research is pleasant but what I read most is undergraduate writing. Instead of marvelling at the burial of Dennis's leg, I excavate graveyards of freshman compositions, getting precious little comfort from comma blunders and dangling modifiers. The ideas and errors of students are remarkably similar, and only wild miswritings are of any interest. "Every family," a Syrian girl wrote, "consisted of a huge number of children, parents, aunts, and angels." Recently a boy wrote a theme for me on "Robinson Caruso." Although I had assigned Defoe's book and the boy obviously had not read it, he passed. The picture I conjured up of Robinson Caruso walking along the beach, gun and umbrella in hand, and singing "Friday, Friday" in a resonant baritone gave me more pleasure than the best-punctuated paper in the class.

Since I do not read for wisdom, I rarely plan my reading far ahead of the present. Instead of reading's determining the way I live, I let reading rise out of living. Like buds in the spring, such reading often starts with little things and then blooms surprisingly bright. In summer, Vicki and I go to Nova Scotia where her parents own an old farm. Built in 1859, the farmhouse is three stories tall and has eleven big rooms and an attic. Back of the house is a meadow overgrown with blueberries and cranberries. On one side of the house wild roses bend under hips and a second blooming; on the other a barn slumps heavily against it. In the barn rusting iron stoves, sleighs, horse collars, and chairs without bottoms tumble together in mounds. The clutter has always dismayed me, and I have never sorted through it. When our little boy Francis first looked inside the barn, though, he yelled in glee. What I thought was trash, he thought was treasure. On rainy days I took him into the barn to play. One chilly afternoon while digging behind a trunk, he pulled out a bundle of newspapers. The papers were brown and tattered, so I looked at them and discovered they were issues of *The Yarmouth Herald* from the years 1862 and 1863. Although the barn was cold, my interest was suddenly hot as I read about the Civil War. On Christmas Day, 1862, *The Herald* described the Confederate victory at Fredericksburg, Virginia. "Stonewall Jackson and the veterans of Cedar Mountain, Bull Run, and Antietam," a correspondent wrote, "were not to be scared by trifles." If news is old enough, I soon read, it becomes new. Often what the world was is more difficult to imagine than what it will become. From today, yesterday's prices seem unbelievable. In 1862 A. J. Hood advertised stoves ranging in price from $3.50 to $50. These, Hood assured readers, came "from the best Foundries." A hundred and twenty years ago, education did not force parents to take out second mortgages. In fall 1863, the Franklin Academy for Young Ladies opened its doors in Yarmouth and announced its fees in *The Herald*. For the eleven week term, tuition was three dollars for girls under ten. For "Junior" girls tuition was four dollars while "Senior" girls paid six. Frills were extra. Drawing cost three more dollars and music seven. Languages were two dollars apiece, and students could choose from Hebrew, Greek, Latin, and French.

In the nineteenth century Yarmouth was a bustling town and merchants filled the *Herald* with advertisements. Half chests of tea—Breakfast, Souchong, Congo, and Oolong— were always for sale. So were apples from New England: Nonpareils, Royal Pippins, Spitzenbergs, Greenings, Baldwins, Concord Pairmins, Bellflowers, Gloria-Mundays, and Newton Pippins. When the Brig Pioneer arrived from Liverpool, Young & Baker announced that for sale at their warehouse were: forty kegs of super carbonate of soda, a cask of house zinc, a half ton of thin sheet lead, sixty bundles of English oakum, ten boxes of Lescher's No. 1 Blue Starch, thirty bags of deck spikes, one hundred and fifteen kegs of the best London lead, a case of Scotch augers, and thirty-five tons of refined and common iron. On New Year's Eve 1862, there was a Promenade Concert. "Under the auspices of the ladies," the concert was held to retire the debt of the Yarmouth Brass Band. Admission was twelve and a half cents. "Vocal and instrumental music" were provided free, but supper and refreshments were additional. The ladies served chicken for supper, or so it seems, for they requested that "Persons intending to make donations of poultry will oblige by handing them in by Monday morning." Although the life described by *The Herald* often appeared quaint and gentle, harsh edges of the age stuck out. "Wanted," a notice read, "Good places for Children, Boys and Girls from one to eight years old—now in the Poor House, to bind out as apprentices."

Down the road from the farmhouse is the Memorial Temperance Hall in which the "Total Abstinence Society" was "instituted" on 25 April, 1828. Early owners of the house had been active in the temperance movement, and Vicki's parents carted a load of temperance hymnals to the dump after they bought the house. New owners, though, are never able to sweep a house clean; remnants of the past always remain. Playing peek-a-boo with me, Francis crawled into an old cupboard in the barn. When I opened the cupboard, I found Francis sitting on copies of *The Tidal Wave* (1874), a temperance hymnal. *Dash It Down, Sign To-Night,* and *Vote It Out,* the songs urged. "Hand not the cup to me," one declared, "When full of death within,/ I ne'er will drink with thee,/ Of brandy, wine or gin." For generations men in my family have enjoyed such cups. My great uncle Earl misbehaved so that he was buried in a lower corner of the family plot, yards away from the rest of the family. In looking into the cupboard, I opened a door not simply to the past but to the present and found matter for an essay. The next morning I began writing an article about the temperance movement, and Uncle Earl and his doings.

In Nova Scotia, days fall into a quiet pattern. I get up

early, make a fire in the stove, and eat a simple breakfast of blueberries, cream, and shredded wheat. After breakfast I make a pot of tea and take it upstairs into a spare bedroom where I write. So that I have time to write, Vicki does not wake Francis until after I am upstairs. One morning, though, while I was writing, the door swung open, and in crawled Francis. When Vicki had gone to the mailbox, he had seized the moment and clambered up the stairs. On the floor of the room lay a long wooden box. Popular novels from the 1920s, two cowbells, a broken brass lamp, and a bucket of sea shells were piled along the top of the box, and I had never opened it. Not satisfied with the dull surface of things, Francis was immediately curious, and after greeting me, began to dig. I tried to continue writing, but when Francis started shaking one of the cowbells, I helped him clear the box. Inside we found sixteen navigation charts published in the 1870s and 1880s. Their owner had marked the voyages he took in pencil. I rolled the charts out on the floor, and pinning the corners down with books, the cowbells, the lamp, began reading. Soon I was sailing through "the Japan Islands," along the "Coast of China," through the "Strait of Sunda and Batavia Bay" to "British Kafraria." The owner of the charts sailed as far as Port Natal, but I never got there. My trips through the South Pacific and the Indian Ocean led me to my grandfather's farm in Virginia where I spent summers as a boy. Kneeling on the floor reading the charts, I remembered running down the attic steps with a top hat or a pair of antlers in my hands. What had happened, I wondered, to that boy? How lost he was in the writing man I had become. As I knelt on the floor with my hands on China and knees on Australia, my mind was on a little Virginia town.

I often think about that town in Virginia, perhaps because I find it difficult to romanticize the present or dream about the future. I read memoirs of southern writers in hopes that their accounts will awaken sleeping memories that I can use in my essays. As much as age, writing has changed the way I read. Instead of books that teach me, I want books that will evoke the tone of past days: the smell of Apinol as I rubbed it into warts on my hands or the taste of a nickel cup of strawberry ice cream just before a storm on a hot summer's afternoon. Travel books also appeal to me now. As I grow older, I enjoy solitude. New experiences hold few charms and strangers seem to have become progressively disgusting or frightening. I have reached a Holiday Inn mentality in which the familiar and expected appeal to me more than the mysterious. Travel books enable me to journey through shadowlands without ever leaving the known world. Like accounts of southern living, they also awaken memories and provide ideas for essays. As I read Paul Theroux's accounts of travels through Europe and across Asia, and later South America, by train, I thought mostly about a trip I made through eastern Europe in the early 1960s. As my train passed through the no-man's land between Austria and Hungary, I looked out the window. There on a watch tower was a guard dancing the twist with his tommy-gun for a partner. On Christmas I arrived in Sofia from Bucharest. Not willing to pay ten dollars for a tourist hotel, I walked the streets until I discovered the World Student Association. Its windows were filled with posters depicting America's exploitation of the world. "Just the group to find a hotel for me," I thought and went in. After I told the director that I was a young communist from the United States, he found me a room for fifty cents a night. For the rest of my travels, I was a communist and my expenses dropped considerably. Nowadays I stay at home and rarely travel. About once a year, though, a shade of the young communist surfaces and I read announcements for academic posts. In hopes of an adventure or at least travelling to a warmer part of the country, I apply. Usually I am interviewed and I leave Hartford feeling young and excited. Like reading a book for truth, though, reading an academic ad for adventure is naive. This past year I visited a university in Georgia. My plane landed at night and a dean picked me up at the airport. For an hour and a half, he drove around in the dark, showing me the town. There were few lights anywhere, and I could distinguish little. Night did not deter the dean, however, and as we drove through the black, he would point out the window and say, "over there is an art center; it's too bad you can't see it." For a while I was irritated, but then suddenly I realized that daylight like solid research would only reveal the ordinary. There in the dark with the dean I was in the wonderful world of Robinson Caruso, the mouse-eating oyster, and Dennis the drummer boy.

Each summer in Nova Scotia, I plan to read little and write a great deal. Alas, a reading man, even if he is on the soft shoulder of time, will always read; even when it is unwanted, reading will spring spontaneously into his day. One morning I took Vicki and Francis for a picnic to Chebogue Cemetery, south of Yarmouth on the coast. The cemetery is on a small hill above a marsh. Like veins on Willow Plate, blue channels run through the marsh, creating a patchwork of small green islands. While Vicki spread a blanket on the ground and unpacked lunch, I explored the graveyard and almost unconsciously began reading the tombstones. Life beside the sea was harsh, and the names of the first settlers of Chebogue were taken from the Old Testament: Silas, Ebenezer, Zilpha, Jeremiah, Moses, Mehetable, Ephraim, Nehemiah, Manassah, and Elkanah. For many life was short. On a weathered stone above eight small markers was the inscription "Our children, white as snow." Above the grave of a four-year-old boy was the epitaph "One less at home! One more in heaven!" I turned away quickly, and seeing Francis at play thanked the Great First Cause that I lived when I did.

The sea brought life and death to Chebogue. Broken white pillars, emblems of men dead before their time, stood throughout the graveyard. On them were inscribed: "Lost at sea, age 23," "Died at St. Domingo," "Lost with twenty-two shipmates on the Wellford," and "Disappeared with the missing ship Dorothy." On 24 February, 1862, Captain Robert MacKinnon and his sons Loran (18) and Charles (16) were lost at sea. Fifteen years later, his son Robert, now 18, disappeared. Then in 1887 his son Joseph (40) was lost. Not until 1904 did Rachel his wife die. Although some women lived long lives, many died young. Childbirth was the woman's sea. Molley Clammans, a stone stated, "Departed this life June 27th 1782, Aged 18 years, 4 Mo & 10 Ds. Also her child who died 4 Days before her, Aged 4 Hours."

Often I look at the books that line my study. They are not arranged in any order. I have moved many times and packing and unpacking have destroyed whatever organization once existed. Like the various people I have been and have forgotten, I cannot recall how my books were arranged. The other day when I had spent a long time looking for a book that I knew was somewhere, a friend said, "this is

stupid; use common sense and organize your books." "Ah,"
I answered and going to *The Last of the Barons* took out a
card. "What the greater part of the world mean by common sense," I read from Hannah More's *Essays*, "will be
generally found, on a closer enquiry, to be art, fraud, or
selfishness! That sort of saving prudence which makes men
extremely attentive to their own safety, or profit; diligent
in the pursuit of their own pleasures; and perfectly at ease
as to what becomes of the rest of mankind." "Hannah
More," my friend exclaimed; "what an old windbag."
"Wind," I said; "listen to this from an eighteenth-century
chapbook" and pulled a card from behind *My Novel.* "A
jovial fellow in Flanders being in bed, let a great fart, and
repeats it twice or thrice; hearing his wife laugh heartily, he
said to her, In troth you need not be so merry, for if this
wind continueth, we are likely to have very foul and filthy
weather.—He falling asleep, she raised her backside, and so
bewatered him that it run from the nape of his neck down
his back to his heels: he awakening, asked what the devil
she meant by that?—Nothing indeed, husband, said she;
for I have heard that a little rain will allay a great wind."

"A scream," my friend said; "I suppose you found that
rank tidbit on one of your research trips." "Right," I said,
"last summer in the British Library." "Why," my friend
said and leaned forward; "why don't you do some useful
research? For that matter make better use not only of your
reading but your life. Everybody has seen you walking
around in the rain picking up worms. What kind of example
are you setting for the students or even your own son? I
have seen him picking up worms with you. Suppose he eats
one—what then?" "Nothing bad will happen to either Francis or the worm," I said; "if you had done your research

and read the issue of *The General Evening Post* for 9 October, 1750," I continued, pulling out a card from behind *What Will He Do With It*, "you wouldn't be so concerned. Just listen to this advertisement. 'WORMS Brought Away *Alive* in the Close-Stool, by the Famous Little Purging SUGAR PLUMS, 12d—a Dozen,' " I read, " 'Or, May but ONE only Sugar PLUM for a PENNY. With Directions With It, Which is Enough to Bring Away WORMS, & Foul Humors, from a Child, Or, To Cure it of a Cough, Or a Fever.' "

Unknown

I'm forty years old and have never met a famous person. No politician has ever shaken my hand or asked for my vote. Although my great-grandfather was a member of the Tennessee legislature, he died long before I was born and I never met him. I wish I had; in pictures he seems a big, friendly man with hands like mittens, and I think I would have liked him. Once an article of mine appeared in *The National Review*, and Bill Buckley sent me a blue card on which he wrote, "Mr. Pickering, Nice Going! Thanks. B." That was the closest I came to Mr. Buckley, and after all, he is not really a politician. Still, I kept his card; it's in my desk in a big, beige envelope along with a few other curiosities of my literary life—a letter, for example, asking if I thought the world as we know it would exist in the year two thousand. The man who wrote the letter wasn't famous, so I answered "yes."

Ten years ago while teaching at University College London, I came close to a famous political theorist. Our acquaintance was a meeting of minds, though, and we didn't shake hands. When Jeremy Bentham died, he left his body to the college, instructing that it be displayed "in the attitude in which I am sitting when engaged in thought." Fully clothed and topped off with a wax head, the skeleton sits comfortably in an exhibition case. Bentham's actual head, however, is stored in a wooden box. Every morning as I walked to my office, I passed the skeleton. If I were in a hurry, I just nodded, but usually I stopped and passing the time of day said good morning or asked after the skeleton's health. After some months I became dissatisfied at not receiving a response and deciding that communication with the rest of the man might be more rewarding, I made arrangements to meet the head. Before I could visit with it, a college official interviewed me twice, just, he said later, "to see if you were hooie." As the official and I lifted the wooden top off the head, a friend who accompanied me jumped up and mumbling something inarticulate ran out of the room. Later I found him sitting on a bench in the main courtyard, his head hanging between his knees and his forehead wet with perspiration. "It's this flu," he said; "I have had it all week."

The head had not aged gracefully, and if my visit with it is typical, then meeting famous people is not very satisfactory. The college official and I, however, got along well. For a long time we talked about "hooie" people. "They are the only ones," he said, "who want to see this head. You should meet them." "Alas," I thought; "I might not have met any famous people but I have attracted hordes of afflicted ones." My childhood is probably to blame. When I was a small boy in the country, I used to play tricks on afflicted people. I meant no harm and at that time thought they liked the attention. They must have not have, though, because ever since they have singled me out for their tricks. Whenever I go anywhere, no matter how I travel, one is nearby. Not long before I met the head I had ridden all night on the bus from Newcastle to London. I was assigned the last vacant seat, one of those in the back over the tires in which a person's knees rest against his nose. On the seat behind sat a girl holding a puppy in her lap. Next to me was a woman on furlough from a sideshow; she was so big that the man who married her would have been guilty of trigamy. Across the aisle on her right was her thirty year old son. He wore a brown suit and a Sherlock Holmes hat and was furiously counting the buttons on his jacket. "Oh, no," I thought, and slumping, tried to curl over the tire. Outside Newcastle the bus hit a pothole and as my knees drove my nose near my eyes, I rose out of hiding. The fat woman slid over, bouncing me against the window. The puppy started barking. Then, woe is me, the afflicted man stood up and bellowed, "Hhormanhuttles, Hhormanhuttles, Hhormanhuttles!" "He is looking at you," his mother said; "he wants you to wave. Wave and he will stop." "What?" I answered, feeling my nose. "For God's sake wave," said a man in front of me; "I want to sleep." Wave, I did—all the long night to London; every time we hit a bump or the puppy barked or whenever the spirit moved him, the poor man yelled and I waved.

Although some are rich, no one I knew in college is famous. Sometimes I wonder if I would meet famous people if I were wealthy. Probably not, even if I did meet them, conversations would likely be shorter than that I had with the head. A well-to-do friend once introduced me to a prominent businessman. The company he owned manufactured clothes and before meeting him, I thought about topics for conversation. Knowing that businessmen were interested in money, I decided to share one of my best schemes with him; and as soon as we were introduced, after looking around to make sure no one could overhear us, I leaned forward and whispered, "you know those preppy shirts that have an alligator on the front." "Yes," he said, stepping back and lifting his drink. "Well," I said, "the way to make a million is to remove the alligator and put a nipple in its place. Every student in the country would buy one. Imagine," I continued, having to raise my voice slightly as he stepped back another step; "imagine the possibilities; nipples here, there, and . . ." Unfortunately I didn't complete the sales talk. The businessman bolted his drink, and muttering something about a refill, rushed to the bar. Things, I suppose, work for the best. The poor man was obviously addicted to alcohol and would have botched the shirts. I tried to talk to him two more times, but each time he gulped down his drink and headed for the bar. Soon he was in no shape for serious business.

Sometimes I dream of being famous. Usually I imagine myself a spy, moving mysteriously through the cool of the evening. I once taught in the Mideast, and when a student asked me if I worked for the C.I.A., I laughed knowingly and said, "you know I can't answer that." For days life seemed intense, and I remained "almost a spy" until summer vacation approached and I suggested to my wife that we go somewhere exciting and have an adventure. "I'm all for that," she said; "give me a suitcase and a Hilton and I'm ready for adventure." Hiltons and adventures rarely meet, and instead of trekking out to the wild unknown, we packed and went home to my family in Nashville, Tennessee. Nothing much happened during our visit except one day I heard a singer on the radio say, "Jesus, when you come, please come to Nashville." "Gosh," I thought, "wouldn't it be something if He did come to Nashville and I met Him. People would really be impressed." "What people," my wife said after dinner that night, "who do you think would stick around? News of his coming would cure every sick person in town. The blind would see and the

lame would walk—at least until they got to Kentucky."
She was right. During the sermon on Sunday when the congregation usually stretches and gossips, I looked around.
With the exception of a car dealer whose business would
have picked up, no one would have been pleased to learn
that the Second Coming was at hand.

Perhaps I am unfair. The preacher might not have been
upset. Yet, at the time, he was rising in the church, and
my guess is that if he had been consulted, he would have
taken a raincheck and put off the Second Coming until he
became a bishop and could have entertained Him in style.
Still, I might be wrong; I have never talked for a long
time to a successful preacher. Once I ate lunch with Oral
Roberts in Tulsa; unfortunately I sat next to Mr. Roberts
and during the fruit cocktail noticed that his fly was un-
zipped. From that moment on I was silent. How, I wondered, all through the meal, was I going to tell Mr. Roberts
about his fly? What would he think about me? After all,
why did I notice it—would he think I was in the habit of
looking into men's laps during lunch? Even worse, because
I had been nervous about eating with Mr. Roberts, I woke
up early that morning. To pass time until lunch, I decided
to explore Tulsa. While driving about the city, I listened to
the radio and from the news learned that a circus was un-
loading at the station. "Oh, boy," I thought, "I'd like to see
that." Since lunch was sometime off, I drove straight to the
station. The first thing I saw was a line of elephants getting
ready to parade through downtown Tulsa. When I was
small, circuses were my great love and all thought of lunch
vanished. Within minutes I was lurching through Tulsa at
the head of the parade. In the fable of the blind men and
the elephant, the blind men quarreled about the elephant's

appearance because each felt a different part of the elephant's body. The blind men used the wrong sense. If they had depended upon smell instead of touch, they would have agreed. Not only does elephant rival skunk in close quarters, but on a hot day its aroma clings close and bores through to soak the skin like ground fog. After eleven blocks, no blind man, no matter how educated his nose, could have distinguished me from the elephant. Since I was wearing my only suit, I couldn't change clothes. When the parade ended, I hurried into a drug store and bought a can of Right Guard. Deodorants, though, are not tested on the creatures of African plain and forest, and although I sprayed my coat and both inside and outside my trousers, the odor of elephant took my breath and during lunch all appetite away.

I have ridden many different animals, and that, I suppose, may be almost as good as meeting famous people. Some years back I spent three days riding camels in Jordan. Unlike foreign cars, foreign animals are not factory-equipped with front wheel drive and are often hard on the operator's rear axle and suspension system. To make me run smoother, I took a fifth of additive along on the trip. At the end of the first day when we reached camp, I opened the additive and soon was well-oiled and idling smoothly. After dinner a companion and I wandered out across the sands and looking at the moon sang of home with its strange-sounding names. Suddenly a shadow broke from the dark about us, and before I could turn to the side, it made my acquaintance and disappeared. The shadow must have been one of our bedouin escorts. Hearing me sing, he probably thought I was famous and wanted to meet me. Bedouins, however, are generally small men, and instead of seizing my hand, the shadow grabbed my drive shaft and squeezed it so hard that he shook me out of high into low gear, where I remained for the rest of the trip.

I spent a year in Jordan and never met anybody famous. Because no prominent people in Amman knew me, I was asked to be Santa Claus at the international community's Christmas party. Although I did not meet their parents, I kissed over two hundred and fifty children, including two of the King's. That's the closest I have ever come to someone famous and I wanted to talk to the children about their father. But when their bodyguards let their machine guns drift toward my chest, my interest in conversation ended abruptly and I ran through the toys and sugar plums as quickly as possible in hopes that at the end of the party St. Nicholas would still be around. Now, as I think back on that evening, I suppose that conversation with the children and even their father would have disappointed me. Famous people have to watch what they say; fame often reduces speech to bland abstractions. No famous person would have written me as did Ibrahim soon after I left Jordan. "University," he began, "has just retraced its steps and started waving the thick stone in our faces. Its doors cracked as opened; its ancient marinars carried their heavy, bright bags under their a little bit bending shoulders, with their glittering eyes hung in their faces. Students stuck to its dusty-iron door, shaking their heads and puffing their cigarittes. Girls passed by and greeted their commarades with heavenly smiles. What a lovely scene! And I with my old memories, along with future hopes shacking up in my mind, drag my footsteps towards a new year of hard work."

I don't think I would gain much from meeting famous people now. So far as I can tell fame leads to conventional behavior. In contrast, ordinary people do extraordinary things. Just the other day I walked out on my deck and looking over into my neighbor's back yard saw him fanning a fire in his barbeque pit. "That won't work," I yelled; "if you want to cool the fire, pour ice water on it." Sometimes I think my neighbor is afflicted. Certainly he is deaf, and when he didn't respond but kept on fanning, I hollared as loud as I could and said, "I'll get a bucket of ice; you wait there." Instead of thanking me, he cursed and told me to stay out of his yard, accusing me of being "in the sauce again." "I don't cook out and would not touch meat sauce. That's for fools who fan fires," I answered and went inside. As usual time proved me right. Fanning didn't cool the fire and ten minutes later the pit was blazing.

On weekends I run road races. I am not fast and during a race I have a lot of time to think. What I used to think about was meeting famous people. Instead of being passed by little girls in alligator shirts and cripples on their way back to Nashville from Kentucky, I dreamed of someone famous drawing alongside and saying, "hello, you look absolutely fascinating. We must talk. What is your name?" For two years I looked carefully at everyone that passed me. No one famous ever appeared. All I met were expressions of the sort Mr. Roberts would have had on his face if he had seen me glancing into his lap. Now, during a race, I rarely think about famous people. To tell the truth I am ashamed of being so slow and hope to do better. If a famous person hailed me, I'd have to break stride and shake hands, and there's no telling where I would finish. The afflicted, I have recently concluded, are the best people to meet during a race. Last fall, I was in a race that crossed the grounds of the state home for retarded adults. The clients, as the state

calls them, danced around and made a fine hullabaloo as we
ran past. Near the end of the race I was worn out and didn't
think I could finish. Just before I collapsed, though, a
cousin of the fellow who travelled with me from Newcastle
to London broke from the ranks of the clients. Waving his
arms and bounding up and down, he approached me and
sticking his face against mine yelled into my ear. I'm not a
linguist and wasn't sure what he said, but I knew he meant
"run fast." And that's what I did. Like Lazarus I found
new energy and streaked off to the finish.

Few people meet as many of the afflicted as I do, and
some like my neighbor probably wouldn't want to meet any.
Still, if one has never met a famous person and would like
to make his life more interesting without cultivating the
afflicted, he ought to try to meet people who have met
famous people. Meeting famous people must resemble total
immersion baptism. Not only is the convert blessed with
the ability to tell outrageous lies, but for the rest of his life
he tries to make others true believers. Fifty years ago the
most famous man in my father's hometown, Carthage, Tennessee, was Abraham Oldacre, a successful, smalltown businessman. Carthage sits on a bluff overlooking the Cumber-
land River. A steel bridge now spans the river, and ten
minutes after turning off the interstate, one can park in
front of the courthouse. Years ago, Carthage was not so
accessible. At the west end of town a toll road stretched
toward Red Boiling Springs. The train station was across
the river, and to reach Carthage, a person had to ride Tolli-
ver's Ferry or use Abraham Oldacre's bridge. The bridge
was a patchwork, wooden affair, but confident that wood
could withstand the wash of water and bring in more money
than metal, Oldacre bought a bus. When a church wasn't

renting it, the bus was parked behind Oldacre's Cafe, just off the square. When the afternoon train arrived, Monroe Dowd took off his apron, closed the cafe and drove across the river to pick up the drummers who had come up from Nashville. A migrant countryman from Defeated Creek, Monroe Dowd marvelled at his employer's success, and before they left the bus, drummers always knew that Oldacre had arrived in Carthage thirty years earlier as a Jewish peddler, carrying pots and pans and a different last name. Now he owned, as Monroe pointed out, the cafe, the bridge, and as some said, part of the variety store and the bank. The ride across the bridge was short, and Monroe told his story rapidly. Rarely were drummers able to interrupt him. One day, however, a drummer sniffing a good marriage behind the peddler's success, managed to force a question into Monroe's narrative. "Did he marry a gentile," the drummer asked. "Oh, no," Monroe answered quickly, eager to run through the list of his employer's properties; "oh, no, he married a Ferguson."

Some time ago a friend asked me to go to a movie with him. "A high school buddy," he said, "is in it. He's on the way to becoming famous, and I want to see what he's like." I agreed to go, and sure enough, my friend's classmate was listed as a character. "Tell me when he appears," I said, settling in with a package of M&M's, a bucket of popcorn, and a coke. "Right," he answered; "I'll nudge you" and sat forward in his seat intensely watching the screen. I didn't come down with indigestion and enjoyed the afternoon. At the end of the film, though, I realized my friend had not nudged me. "Hey," I said, "you forgot to point out your buddy." "Not—not exactly," answered, "I didn't recognize him. Anyway," he added as we left the theater, "we weren't really very good friends." Like Monroe's account which entertained in itself and did not make one want to meet Abraham Oldacre, so the movie was good and I didn't mind missing the almost-famous classmate. Not long after we saw the movie, however, the classmate landed a role in a television serial. The serial became successful and the classmate is now famous. Last summer I went to a barbeque at my friend's house, and while I grazed on crackers and onion dip, I heard him talking about his classmate. "We were great friends," he said; "played on the same high school football team. I was first string and he was a substitute, but that didn't make any difference because I liked him. Once we took out two girls from another school, and he told them that we were both on the all-city team. By the end of the evening we had those girls in the palms of our hands—so to speak. On the way home, I said to him, 'Preston, you ought to be an actor.' 'Hadn't thought about it, Harold,' he answered, 'but maybe I will.'" Suddenly the onion dip seemed bland, and before Harold saw me, I headed for the bar and something highly seasoned.

Nowadays I don't think as much about meeting famous people as I once did. Monroe Dowd's descendants almost satisfy me. Of course, if my neighbor moved away I might be happier. He is a businessman and when I told him about my idea for putting nipples on shirts, he called me a "nut" and told me to get out of his yard. I got back at him though. One afternoon I watched him fan a fire in his barbeque pit for almost fifteen minutes, and when he went inside the house for the meat, I poured a bucket of water over the fire. He thought I did it but couldn't prove it. "I'll fix your little red wagon," he said. "Be careful," I answered, thinking of those days when I almost worked for the C.I.A.; "before you do anything you better find out what I did before I came here. Don't say later that I didn't warn you."

Occasionally, though, I imagine meeting a famous person. This past spring I attended a performance of *The Merry Widow*. Midway, as the orchestra played "The Merry Widow Waltz" and couples spun like dolls across the stage, the woman in front of me stood, turned around, and after fixing me with a dark eye, shouted, "I'm the Merry Widow; it's my birthday. Look at me." Although I once dated a girl who was Miss U.S.A. Sugar Cane, I had never really met a famous woman, much less one who had an opera named after her. "Holy cow," I thought, "should I introduce myself." Before I could decide or even put my opera glasses in their case, the woman toppled forward across her seat, and began to moan. Instead of being Lehar's inspiration, she was one of the afflicted. As the ushers led her away, I felt disappointed. "I guess I never will meet anyone famous," I thought gloomily. But as the opera swung to a merry conclusion, I brightened. "If that's so, then no one famous will ever meet me; too bad for them," I thought and left the theater whistling.

Upstairs

Although I grew up in Nashville and my parents still live in our old house, I don't visit much now. Eastern Connecticut is a long way from Middle Tennessee, almost as far, it sometimes seems, as forty-five is from twenty. This past summer, though, with my wife Vicki and our two little boys, I flew to Nashville. Mother keeps our house spotless, and after dinner the first night, I strolled through all the rooms. Things were in their places. The silver was shined and the tables waxed. Not a single portrait was askew and all the rugs were flat on the floor. Even mother's plants seem to grow with cool regularity and decorum, and for a while I was comfortable. That night, however, my thoughts began to roam beyond the cleanly-ordered public display of the rooms, and I had trouble sleeping. The next morning after breakfast, I went upstairs. There in the hot dusty attic where racks of old clothes leaned together in aisles, and trunks, warped shoes, and Windsor chairs were gathered in mounds was another world, one far less congenial than that below but one that had a greater power.

During the two weeks we were in Nashville, I went upstairs every morning. My trips to the attic did not last long; by noon the heat like my past became too much to bear and I was happy to return to the air-conditioning downstairs. What I had become determined what I saw in the attic. Since I am a bookish person I paid little attention to boxes filled with linen and lace. Instead I was drawn to scrapbooks and cases of letters, some of them old and some of them mine. Quilts, camisoles, and christening gowns did not interest me when I rummaged through the trunks; only when I found hairbrushes and mirrors wrapped in newspapers did I pause. Carefully I peeled away the papers, not concerned about things protected but about what the papers revealed about life in the small towns from which my ancestors came. And I suppose I also wanted to know about myself; why despite many opportunities I have made so little of my life and when real success has come to my front door have I always fled out the back, seeking anonymity and quiet. I spent one morning reading remnants of the *Record-Democrat* published in Carthage, Tennessee, in 1894. The margins of the paper interested me more than the body, and I ignored the headlines and read notes like "W. N. Adams asked us to say that he will be on his round at the usual time this spring castrating colts" and "Dick Hodges lost a fine hog Sunday with cholera." My great-grandfather William B. Pickering founded the Methodist Church in Carthage, and I wondered what he thought about the Reverend Sam P. Jones who said, "It don't take much to make a good average Methodist. Go to church once a week, give about one-tenth of what you should, and keep out of the penitentiary."

One of the fictions that those of us who don't quite fit the world console ourselves with is that our childhoods were unhappy. Often I have heard someone say that he was always the last person chosen for teams and as a result suffered terribly as a child. I have said it many times myself, but I lied. In truth my childhood was gloriously happy, and the big, thick scrapbooks that mother kept for me overflow with memorabilia of a boy who was ever-popular and lovingly nurtured. Mother held on to everything: my first airplane ticket for a flight in June 1943, and from Bessie Braxton, a country girl that played with me when I was little, a letter which began "I was very sory to heur about you burt yurself." Mother even kept the bill for my birth at Vanderbilt Hospital. Unlike Edward, my second son, who was a thirty-seven hundred dollar baby, I cost sixty-five dollars and twenty-five cents.

In the scrapbooks were years of letters from my grandfather, my mother's father, and his brothers in Virginia. Shortly after I was born, Uncle Wilbur wrote, "Enclosed you will find a check. At present it will be of little value to you but as time goes on it will come in handy for nothing but ice cream cones. Don't let anyone kid you about saving it. You only save it until you get to the ice cream stage and then you have a good time. I would not advise using it all at once; it would probably be better to take at least one or two weeks for the ordeal." Some years later Uncle Harold asked, "What in the world are you doing sick! Here, I have been waiting all the winter for you to finish school and come up and take over my sheep. I am sending you $5.00 advance payment on your wages and am expecting you here just as soon as school is over, so don't you let me down."

Until his death my grandfather wrote splendid letters. "It has been a very long time since I have seen you, and I miss you very much," he began just before my fourth birthday; "I hope you will have a fine birthday, and I am sure you will have, and I am going to try and ship you two wild cats—very large ones, and if the man on the train will take them, they will be in a cage, and they should get to Nashville about the time of your birthday, but I am afraid they are going to kill everybody in Nashville, because they are very wild and vicious." "I killed seven wolves the other night," grandfather continued; "they most chewed a little boy up, but we got him to the hospital, and he is all right now, and if these wild cats do not kill everybody in Nashville, I will send two large wolves that will, so you had better tell your Mother about this at once to see whether she wants them sent down, because I do not want to build a cage for these wolves and wild cats until you have got some place to put them." After describing "the biggest snake you ever saw" and the pumas that were "scared to death" of him, grandfather ended, writing, "the brown cow bull asks every day if you are still drinking your milk, and I told him that you were a very good boy and I felt sure you were drinking your milk and behaving yourself like a man, because you know we men have to stick together."

Written to an only child who lived in a city but who dreamed about summers in the country, grandfather's letters were exciting and loving. Indeed, more than anything else, attics are testimonials to affection. From Bibles swollen with forget-me-nots to stacks of Valentines, attics contain countless tokens of affection. On the frontispiece of Stephen Foster's *Plantation Melodies*, I read, "To Miss Courtny, May the angels of peace ever cluster around you and quiet you. Your absent friends, Confederate soldiers, C. C. Cauthorn, Maj. Cauthorn Jones." In a young, bold hand, far different from that now shrunk by time, father sent mother his guest list for their wedding. "Sweetheart," he wrote, "Heah it is—Isn't it neat. Will add a few names later. Sam." Perhaps the reason why those of us who were popular, loved children say that our childhoods were unhappy is that love complicates life and brings suffering. Forgetfulness is one of life's blessings; without it few people would be able to endure. Remembrances of loves past brings guilt and because they did not last an aching sense of things missed. As I dug through the clutter in the attic, so parts of my forgotten life appeared.

When I found the box of letters from Annie my first love, I wanted to return to the ordered emotions downstairs. There with my children were the actual and the present. I knew that reading Annie's letters would stir my emotions and could be seen simply as the attempt of a bored, middle-aged man to titillate himself—as perhaps were all my explorations upstairs. Rationally I knew that Annie now had to be an ordinary person like me with a station wagon, two children, and an aquarium teeming with guppies. And yet the picture of a bright and warm young woman with her life all before her and me smiling at her side would not go away, and so I read. Four pages into a letter in a discussion of a college philosophy course, Annie stopped abruptly. "My dear Sam," she began, "I am quite certain that I am carrying your child. I have not yet decided what to do. Ironically I have never felt so alone in my life. I know that pre-marital intercourse itself is not the greatest sin; I shall never condemn the emotion that caused it. The sin for which I am suffering most is my failure to obey the law which commands to honor thy Father and Mother. It would not be so hard on me if I did not love them so much. I have not the courage yet to tell them. I shall have to soon. I think I will go home next weekend; it will be the hardest trial of my life. I want to be such a credit to them and I have failed them. Sam, please know that I will understand whatever your response will be to this letter; I will also understand if the response does not come right away."

As I sat grieving for the child not born and the years that

Annie and I did not share, I heard my children outside. They wanted me to come down and play, but the attic held me and I remembered a dream that awakened me early on the morning of that day when Annie's child would have been born. In the dream I was walking in a forest with my infant son. I had to go to work, so I wrapped him for his safety in swaddling clothes and left him in a cabin by a lake. The work lasted longer than I had expected, and when I returned late to the cabin, I heard the baby crying. "He is crying," I thought, "because he has soiled himself." I was wrong. When I opened the cabin door, the child looked at me in terror and shrieked, "Don't kill me! Don't kill me!"

Upstairs is personal. Attics record the lives of individuals, not nations. Alongside the marks left by a forgotten person, the way of a nation seems unimportant and history fades into an abstraction. What was striking in a biography of Lincoln published in 1865 was not the account of the Civil War or the celebration of Lincoln, whose name, the author wrote, "will be perennial as the sun"—no, more memorable and touching were the sketches of small girls in long dresses, drawn throughout the book by some child whose identity has vanished. Although the times in which one lives influence life, what often remains in an attic is not the age but the individual. Even during turmoil of the Civil War, glimpses of individuals stood out and to later generations are more alive than historical fact. In a box I found several albums containing sheet music. In one was the music to "How Are You, John Morgan," a comic song published in Kentucky in 1864 and describing the capture of the famous Confederate raider. With a frontispiece depicting Morgan riding a mule, the song was appealing as an artifact or conversation piece. My great-grandmother Nannie Brown had changed the words, however, and brought the song and herself to life. On the first page Nannie drew a line through "John Morgan's caught" and above it wrote "he's made his escape." Near the end she changed "into prison cast" to "in the Dixie State." I spent much time reading the songs published during the War, in part I suppose because people in Connecticut forever ask me where I am from and never let me live in an ordered downstairs, apart from place and personality. In 1861, "Missouri! or a Voice from the South" urged secession, pleading with Missourians to "add your bright Star to our Flag of Eleven." The War did not bring immediate change, and the publishers of "Missouri!" A. E. Blackmar & Bro. of New Orleans advertised their music, saying "Dealers and Schools supplied at the old Northern Rates."

As many items in the attic were devoted to love so much pertained to music. Under a beam, I found Tex Ritter's recordings of my childhood favorites, "Billy, the Kid" and "The Phantom White Stallion of Skull Valley." Nearby were father's records, songs like "Alice Blue Gown," "Indian Love Call," and "From the Land of Sky Blue Water." During the nineteenth century girls in my family collected music like I collected baseball cards in the 1950s. Attics are the tombs and preservers of sentiment; in them we store memories and build mausoleums out of memories that we dare not erect in public. Upstairs one can sentimentalize safely, and the titles of the music made me imagine a world in which I would be more comfortable. Time and this life passed quietly away as I read "Mary of the Wild Moor," "Are We Almost There," "The Giraffe Waltz," "The

Wrecker's Daughter Quick Step," and "Be Kind to the Loved Ones at Home."

Downstairs reason returned, and I realized my pastoral vision was silly. Amid the light and sentimental tunes was "General McClellan's March," published in Ohio in 1864. Indeed emblems of violence were scattered throughout the attic. These ranged from toy soldiers and cannon that had been manufactured in France and Great Britain before World War I to a box of cap pistols, each with a name on the butt: Presto, Champion, Long Tom, and Texan, Jr. In a case was a collection of guns, two rifles manufactured in Danzig in 1915, several twenty-twos, and various shotguns with which I once hunted. Opening the case, I took out the guns, examined the firing mechanisms, tested the balances, and then one by one pointed them out a window and snapped off imaginary shots. It had been a long time since I held a gun. Some years ago in New Hampshire, the feelings of aggression and depression that occasionally sweep over me so frightened me that I broke the shotgun I hunted with down into parts. Since the house I was living in did not have an attic, I carried the parts into the basement and locked each in a separate trunk. The basement was damp; the parts rusted, and when I left New Hampshire, I threw the gun away.

Attics are deceptive. Although one wants to believe that their clutter can reveal identity, it may be more accurate to think that sight is selective and that we see what we want to see. Nevertheless upstairs made me think that my feelings about guns and violence had been ambivalent for a long time. Mother kept my first-grade notebooks. Among the arithmetic and spelling exercises were coloring books. I was born just before World War II and many of my pictures reflected the war. In these flights of bombers sank tons of ships. Always black or brown, all the ships flew the Rising Sun. The planes were more colorful with, for example, orange bodies and red wings or blue bodies and yellow wings. In contrast to the ships, they did not fly a national emblem; instead on the side of each I drew flowers—awkward, sprawling daisies.

Psychology strikes me as absurd, and I have often mocked its pretentions. Actually, if heredity has much to do with development, my lack of sympathy for psychology may reflect an inability to understand. In the attic I discovered my father's grades at Vanderbilt. During 1927–28, he took three courses in psychology and made three Ds. Whatever the flowers on the planes reveal about me, if anything, however, an attic can help one cope with life. My older boy Francis is three years old, and I am worried about him. He is not like other boys his age. He is more awkward than they are, and he stutters badly. When children come to our house, they ignore him and instead play with his younger brother Edward, who is hardy and bright and rushes heedlessly about shouting and laughing. For a while Francis watches Edward and visitors, eager to be part of the play. But no matter how he tries, he does not fit in, and eventually he goes off by himself.

In Nashville, two boys from next door came over to play. Although Francis was obviously happy to see them, they ignored him and played with Edward. Flowers are Francis's great love, and he spends hours smelling, and then looking at them and the bees that buzz around them. When the children refused to acknowledge him, Francis picked a Gerber daisy from mother's flower bed. Silently he approached the boys and holding the flower tenderly, showed it to them. Nothing that Francis could have done would have interested the boys, and they only glanced at the flower and said nothing. For a minute Francis held the flower out expectantly; then slowly, he tore it into pieces. The picture of a lonely, inarticulate little boy destroying the thing he loved seemed to foreshadow years of unhappiness, and I became terribly sad, then angry—angry at life for making a child so unhappy. But later upstairs made everything right. In a scrapbook I found several pictures of my grandfather Ratcliffe, that kind, well-adjusted man who wanted to send me wolves and wildcats. Taken in 1892, one of the pictures was of pupils in a one-room school in Mechanicsville, Virginia. My grandfather was the youngest and smallest of the twenty-three children. Barefoot and wearing trousers which gathered and buttoned just below the knee, he sat on a bench at the end of the front row. Between him and the boy next to him was a space, the only space between students in the picture. In his hands, grandfather held a clump of flowers, and on his face was my son's sad expression. "That's him," I said aloud; "that's Francis; everything is going to work out."

Two years ago during a visit to her parents, Vicki and I went to their attic to find playthings for Francis. Vicki's favorite toy had been a Teddy Bear named Nurse Woolly. Inside Nurse Woolly was a music box, and when Vicki found Nurse Woolly in the attic, she wound her up. The bear played—but only once. At the end of the song, there was a pinging sound and a spring burst out under Nurse Woolly's arm. Like winding that Teddy Bear the attempt to capture what one imagines as the splendor of childhood is futile. Yet people try, especially as they grow older and less able to imagine a happy future. Although my motives are now obscured by what I found, I initially went upstairs to get toys for Francis and Edward. Or so I said; I suppose, though, I went like Vicki, looking for my own Nurse Woolly and hoping to hear the forgotten melodies of childhood. From my children's point of view, my explorations upstairs were a success. I brought down a box of books, a large green and yellow "Ice Buddy Truck," and a Wyandotte convertible with a retractable metal roof.

One of the books described the adventures of a toy tugboat, named Scuffy. Bored by life in a bathtub, Scuffy escaped from his owners, a man in "a blue polka-dotted tie" and his son. Floating along creeks and small rivers, through farms and woodlands, and past deer and cattle, Scuffy was happy at first. But then as the river grew larger and Scuffy saw large cities and approached the wide sea, he became frightened and wished he were back at home. In children's books, one can always return home, and just as he was being swept out into the sea, the man in the blue polka-dotted necktie reached out from a pier, plucked Scuffy out of the water, and took him back to a happy life in the bathtub. Unlike the heroes and heroines of children's books, the main character in an adult's life cannot return home after floating through years of experiences. And if he tries, he will discover that those things which once delighted him and which he remembers fondly will delight him no more.

One of the trunks upstairs contained games, Scrabble, Monopoly, Parcheesi. Once I enjoyed Parcheesi; now I don't know the rules. Games don't interest me. Age has made me cautious, and as I labor to block chance out of my life, spinning wheels and dice seem frightening emblems of the unknowns that lie ahead and threaten me and my family. As I no longer enjoy games, so I do not play practical jokes. Years ago when the future seemed bright and filled with laughter, I enjoyed jokes. In the trunk with the games, I found a postcard which I mailed to some fifteen of Nashville's most successful businessmen from Bulgaria in 1964. On the front of the postcard was the Soviet Victory Monument in Sofia; on the back I wrote, "Greetings for new year. I remember old days when you would stand in fraturnity hawse and say, from each according to ability—to each according to need. You had such hopes for 1930s. Now the time has come. Shed your skin and shew your true colour. All have hopes for you. Andrei." As I read the card I cringed; yet I felt loss and wondered what had turned that silly boy into such a conventional man.

During the early 1950s, baseball cards were the passion of my life, and eagerly I hunted for my collection, expecting something magical to happen when I found it. I had many cards and players from teams which no longer exist: the Philadelphia Athletics, Boston Braves, St. Louis Browns, and Washington Senators. When I eventually unearthed the collection, I was disappointed. Nothing happened; on top of the collection was a notebook in which I had listed the cards I owned. The care with which I amassed statistics amazed me. I listed every player I had on two or more teams, some two hundred and thirty-six. I even wrote down the percentages of each type of card in my collection. Thus on 12 June 1956, twelve percent of my collection were "Old Topps" while "TV" cards made up seven percent and Topps from 1955 constituted ten percent. Before I found the collection, I imagined that players' names would awaken happy associations, but I never looked at the cards. I wasn't even curious. Instead I examined the cigar boxes in which they were packed—Garcia Delight, Tampa Nugget, and El Trelles with their orange suns, long beaches, palm trees, and dark-eyed smokey maidens.

Before I left Nashville, I packed four trunks and shipped them to Connecticut. When they arrive, I will take them upstairs. I won't open them; someday, though, maybe Francis or Edward will investigate. There is a pile of blocks in the attic and on cool days the boys already like to go upstairs and build forts then run about and hide behind the clothes and boxes. When I was in the hospital in 1948 to have my tonsils removed, I made drawings for my great-uncles. "I have your letter with the fish and hat," Uncle Walter wrote back; "frankly I have never seen a fish before with a hat on, and this is the best I will ever see. I want to congratulate you on such a fine drawing." Although he did not know what to make of my drawing, Uncle Walter's response was just right. Someday my boys will go upstairs, not to play but because something in life made them go. When they look into the trunks I have stored there, they will be puzzled. Amid the clutter they will see fishes wearing hats, things which will make them pause then wonder about themselves and the generations who have disappeared to the upstairs.

Composing a Life

Last month I received a letter that began, "Are you the Samuel Pickering that went to Sewanee twenty years ago?" I did not know how to answer the letter. A boy with my name once attended college at Sewanee, and although I knew him fairly well and think I liked him that boy had long since disappeared. Some good things happened to him at college, and I have often considered writing about them. The trouble is that I am not sure if the things I remember actually happened. Did that boy actually carry a hammer into Professor Martin's class one day, and when an old roommate Jimmy asked why he had it, did that boy really say "for nailing hands to desks." And did he tell Jimmy to flatten his hand out on the desk if he did not believe him—whereupon trusting a friend Jimmy did so. Shortly afterwards when Professor Martin asked Jimmy why he had screamed, did Jimmy answer, "Pickering hit me with a hammer"? And did that boy stand up and say, "I cannot tell a lie; I hit him with my little hammer."

No, no—the person who I have become certainly didn't do that. This person lives in a world without Jimmys, hammers, screams, and exclamation points. For fifteen years I have taught writing. For ten of these years writing has taught me, and I have labored not so much to compose sentences as to compose my life. Hours at the desk and countless erasures have brought success. I haven't committed a comma blunder in almost five years, certainly not since I married my second wife. Happily I have forgotten what participles and gerunds are, but then I have forgotten most things: books, loves, and most of my identities. At my dining room table, dangling modifiers are not mentioned, and I ignore all question marks as my days are composed, not of lurid prose and purple moments, but of calm of mind and forthright, workaday sentences.

Rarely do I use a complex sentence, and even more rarely do I live with complexity. In a simple style I write about simple people, people born before the first infinitive was split and the wrath of grammarians fell upon mankind. Occasionally I write about a small town in Virginia where I spent summers as a boy. In the center of the town was the railway station. Clustered about it were the bank and post office, Ankenbauer's Cafe and Horace Vickery's store. Mr. Vickery was a big man; alongside him, his wife, whom he called "Little Bitty Bird," seemed no larger than a sparrow. Mrs. Vickery spent her days in the domestic nest over the store where she delighted in rearranging furniture. One night Mr. Vickery returned home late from a meeting of the Masons; and if the truth be known, he came home a trifle "happy." Not wanting to wake Mrs. Vickery, he did not turn on the bedroom light. He undressed in the dark and after hanging his clothes up, silently slipped into his pajamas then leaned over to get into bed. Alas, the bed was not where he remembered it; Mrs. Vickery had spent the evening moving furniture, and as Mr. Vickery reached to pull back the covers, he fell to the floor in a great heap. "Oh, Little Bitty Bird," he sang out once he got his breath, "what have you done?"

By rearranging her few possessions Mrs. Vickery was able to create new worlds for herself. Distant places did not

appeal to her, and when her husband took the day train to
Richmond, seventeen miles away, she stayed home, content
to shift a chair or dresser. As I think about Mrs. Vickery
now, her life seems almost ideal. In my seven years in
eastern Connecticut, I have lived simply, rarely traveling to
Hartford thirty miles away. Years ago simplicity held little
attraction for me, and I traveled far afield seeking the confusion of mixed metaphors and long, run-on sentences.
Dashes marked my days, and I dreamed of breaking
through the tried and the safe into the unknown. Once in
Baku on the Caspian Sea, Soviet police dogged my footsteps, and I retreated into the twisting byways of the old
town where I would suddenly disappear and then just as
suddenly reappear, much to my pleasure and, as I thought,
to the amazement of the police. When I began to write, I
was taught to vary my style. "Use different sentence struc-
tures; be different people," teachers told me. And for a
while I did that, meandering along slowly then darting
forward only to turn back abruptly like the boy in Baku.
Here I would insert a compound sentence, there a noun
clause, here a grey man of mystery, there a colorful ec-
centric. For years experimenting was good, and although I
didn't publish much, I had many styles and identities. Now
the older and simpler me stays home, and as my car is a
family station wagon—an American made Plymouth Re-
liant—I have only one style, the solid, economical, fifty-
thousand mile warranteed reliable style of the short declarative sentence.

Other kinds of sentences offend me and seem unsound
and unsettling. Words, rules, and life confuse people. The
simple style orders confusion, at first producing the illusion
of control and then, after time, the reality. When pressure

makes a person bear down so hard that he or his pencil breaks, he should struggle to write simply. By doing so one can regain composure. For years shots made me faint, and I shuddered whenever I entered a doctor's office. Then one day I found myself in a small room waiting for a blood test while another man sat on a couch outside. When the nurse appeared and saw me and the man outside, she called a companion on the telephone. "Mary," she said, "you better come down. There's two here waiting to be stuck. I'll stick the one inside, and you stick the one outside." What a wondrously insensitive thing to say, I thought, certain I would soon topple over. I was wrong; suddenly my nervousness vanished as I pondered sticking the nurse's remarks into an article I was writing. And that shot and those that have followed have passed without a tumble. Thoughts about writing never fail to contribute to my composure. Whenever I visit a doctor now, I don't walk into his office trembling in expectation of the worst sort of parsing. Instead I am ready to turn the experience into a story and thus control it. Once while in the Mideast, I picked up an exotic fungus. Although the fungus was out of sight, it grew on a part of my body that made me uneasy, and as soon as I returned to Connecticut I went to a dermatologist. "Good God," he exclaimed when I showed the fungus to him; "I have never seen anything like that." Then pausing for a moment, he added cheerfully, "all I can say is that I am glad it is on you and not on me."

I am not always successful in composing things. Sometimes words get out of hand and carrying me beyond the fullstops I plan spill over into the tentative world of the colon and expose parts of life that ought to remain buried. Some time ago I decided to write about my summers in

Virginia. The essay didn't turn out to be the hymn to golden days that I envisioned. When it appeared in print, I read it and was disturbed. None of my periods worked. "Good country people," the essay began, "scare the hell out of me. Once I liked the country and thought that the closer a person was to the soil, the nearer he was to God. I know better now. The closer a person is to the soil, the dirtier he is." The essay bothered me until I read a note a boy handed in with a story he wrote as an assignment for a course I teach in children's literature. The students were told to write cheerful stories with positive endings. "I am sorry this is such a terrible story," the boy explained, "but I just couldn't think of a good one. They all kept coming out the other way around with Evil triumphing. I am a very disobedient person by nature." All people and sentences are disobedient; and after reading the note, I realized that words like human beings occasionally violated the best outlines. All one could do was erase, rewrite, and hope that evil would not triumph in the final draft.

As a person has to struggle with words to make them obedient, so one has to revise life. The effort to become simple and perhaps boring is difficult, but I am succeeding. At least twice a week I tell my wife Vicki that she is fortunate to be married to such a conventional person. "Stop saying the same simple-minded things," she replies; "you are hopelessly repetitive." "Ah, ha," I think, "a few more years and my fullstops will block everything unsettling." In passing, I should add that as one grows older and better able to master simple thoughts, he will, nevertheless, violate many rules of grammar. I, for example, am over forty and don't have the energy I once had. Despite suggestions that urge me to use the active rather than the passive voice, I am afraid I live in the passive. Let young writers attempt to manage lively active verbs and do all sorts of creative things to predicates. For my part I am content to be acted upon. Occasionally I ponder taking a forceful part in life but the fit passes. As one grows older, material goods become less important; as one learns the virtues of the oblique approach, direct objects disappear from life.

Age has taught me the value of a familiar, relaxed style and life, beyond direct objects. On weekends I run races. My goal is never to complete a race in the first fifty percent of the finishers. Unlike top road racers, my performance never disappoints me. Sometimes I am tempted to thrust ahead but I always resist. Last weekend as I trotted down a street, a young woman yelled, "you are so cute." To be honest, after hearing that I heisted my legs up a bit and pranced for a while, but then as soon as I was around the corner and out of sight, I settled back into a slow, comfortable rhythm and let a crowd of younger active runners rush by, chasing celebrity and trophies.

Age and the experience it brings lead a person to break many grammar rules. Students in my writing classes always confuse *its* the possessive with *it's* the contraction. When I first began to teach, I railed against the error, attributing ignorance about the possessive to a left-wing conspiracy that was sweeping the nation and undermining the concept of private property. Nowadays I don't give a hoot about the possessive, in great part because I no longer have anything that is mine and mine alone. My two little boys, aged three and one, have converted me to socialism, something no learned text or philosopher was able to do. What I once thought belonged to me, I now realize is theirs too. My papers are pushed aside and my desk has become a parking lot for Corgi Juniors, Hot Wheels, and Matchbox cars. At night Vicki and I don't sleep alone; we share our bed with an ever-changing group of visitors including Little Bear, Big Bear, Green Worm, and Blue Pillow.

Like a good essay, the composed life has a beginning, middle, and definite ending. Youth can dream about the future and imagine a multitude of endings, and as a result usually can't write well. After forty, dreams stop and one buys life insurance. Instead of evoking visions of idyllic pleasure, the ellipsis that looms ahead leads only to an erasure and an empty notebook. For the writer beyond forty the end is clear and nothing can change it. In contrast the past is infinitely malleable, and I often write about it, trying to give shape to fragments that cling to memory. In classes I tell students to write about the small things in the first paragraph of life and not worry about the conclusion. It will take care of itself. All writers should avoid shadowlands where things are not clear and simple. Occasionally, the complex and mysterious tempt me, and I consider writing about such things as a train journey I made on Christmas Eve, 1964, from Bucharest to Sofia. Guards with tommy guns paced up and down inside the cars while outside the train whistle blew hauntingly through the night. Near the Bulgarian border snow began to fall, and I joined a funeral party that was drinking sorrow away. At the border when guards began to pull people roughly from the train, I opened the window in my compartment and serenaded them with Christmas carols. I got through "Hark the Herald Angels Sing" and was just beginning "The First Noel" when a somber man entered the compartment and grabbing my jacket, pulled me back inside to the seat. Without saying anything, he sat next to me. The funeral party looked at him, then left, and the two of us rode all the way to Sofia in silence. I often wonder what went through the man's mind as we travelled through Christmas morning together. Yet whenever I begin to speculate, my thoughts soon turn toward summers and trains in Virginia. Men sat on the porch of Vickery's store, and as the trains passed through, said things that I remembered, simple things that now seem more important and more lasting than all the mysterious silences I have known. "She's a long one," someone would invariably say about a slow freight; "on the way to Richmond," somebody would add. Toward evening when the coal train to Fredericksburg was due, a man was sure to look at his watch and say "about time for the coal train." "And for my dinner," someone else would say and then get up and start home.

The reading I assigned students in writing courses once created a difficulty for me. Anthologies always contain a few pieces by well-known writers, people that students will hear about someday. Setting myself up as an authority when I was unknown bothered me. Even worse I knew I would always be unknown. Aside from writing an essay that would find its way into an anthology and thrust me out of anonymity, something that was impossible for a person so passive, I didn't know what to do. A little thought and some labor at revising, however, worked a change. I wrote a piece in which I celebrated anonymity and as a consequence am now wonderfully content. Oddly enough, being unknown and being satisfied with a passive, simple style has brought me attention. Not long ago the *Willimantic Chronicle,* our local newspaper, began an article on road racing by quoting me. Unfortunately, or perhaps fortunately, for fame can disrupt a simple style, the article began with a typographical error. "Ass Sam Pickering has noted," the paper stated—I have forgotten the rest. After such a beginning, it seems unimportant.

A problem arises after one turns life into a series of balanced, short declarative sentences. Well-placed modifiers and proper subordination do not lend themselves to startling essays. The run-on life, like the sentence, breaks through propriety and occasionally stumbles into interesting constructions. I wondered if I would be able to write once my sentences were under control and my life simple. I should not have worried. Almost every day the postman brings me matter for essays. "Good going old horse," a former student wrote after he read something of mine. "My Dear Samuel Pickering, Jr, I have read your brilliant book and found great satisfaction in it," a woman wrote after reading an article of mine in a quarterly. "Our universe is rolling on in an endless chain of miseries and misfortunes," a man wrote from Syria; "it is the law of our land that we all should die one day; we die when children, money, profession, fame either, can do us nothing. We stand alone, stripped out of everything, in a contest, without spectators, without glamour and hope of win or fear of loss—with much delight and disbelief in our competitor's right and still less confidence in ours. My father died 20 days ago dreaming in the world to come."

As transitions link fragments of life and enable one to escape despair, that terrible sense that nothing matters and chance determines everything, so they bind my disparate letters into articles. Many years ago, before the first sentence of my life was conceived, my grandfather owned a dairy. Although grandfather had several businesses, Henry Hackenbridge his herdsman assumed the dairy was the most important. Every day Henry came to grandfather's house and in great detail described the mood of the herd. When grandfather went out of town, Henry wrote him letters daily. Once after breakfast at the old Ritz in New York, grandfather went to fetch his letter. "Yes, sir, Mr. Ratcliffe, there is something for you," the clerk said and started to hand grandfather a letter. Suddenly a look of concern came over his face, and he said, "oh, dear, I am so sorry." Grandfather was puzzled until he saw the letter. Under the address in big, clear letters, Henry had written, "P.S. Grandma slipped last night." Although the clerk did not know it, Grandma was not my grandfather's mother or wife. She was an old cow, and the night before she had not fallen on the stairs or in the hall, but had in the language of the dairy, lost her calf. When I search for the right transition, I often think of this story. If I can find the right word and am able to keep my life and sentences simple, chances are good that I won't slip too often.